ROBERT AND LOUISA STEWART

In Life and in Death

"They were lovely and pleasant in
their lives, and in their death they were
not divided."—2 Sam. i. 23

BY

MARY E. WATSON

Sister of Mrs. Stewart)

WITH A CHAPTER BY

Mr. EUGENE STOCK

WITH SIX ILLUSTRATIONS AND A MAP.

FOURTH EDITION.

London

MARSHALL BROTHERS

KESWICK HOUSE, PATERNOSTER ROW, E.C.

MDCCCXCV

<u>Printing Statement:</u>

Due to the very old age and scarcity of this book,
many of the pages may be hard to read due to the
blurring of the original text, possible missing pages,
missing text, dark backgrounds and other issues
beyond our control.

Because this is such an important and rare work, we
believe it is best to reproduce this book regardless of
its original condition.

Thank you for your understanding.

PREFACE

HAVING been asked to write a brief memoir of our dear brother and sister, and to give some details of their life-work, I have complied with the request.

As a first effort by one who makes no claim to literary gifts, I must ask a generous forgiveness for all faults of style.

If any one is encouraged by reading the story to "go and do likewise" in the great Mission Field, my reward will be ample.

M. E. W.

CONTENTS

CHAPTER VIII.

CHAPTER IX.

CHAPTER X.

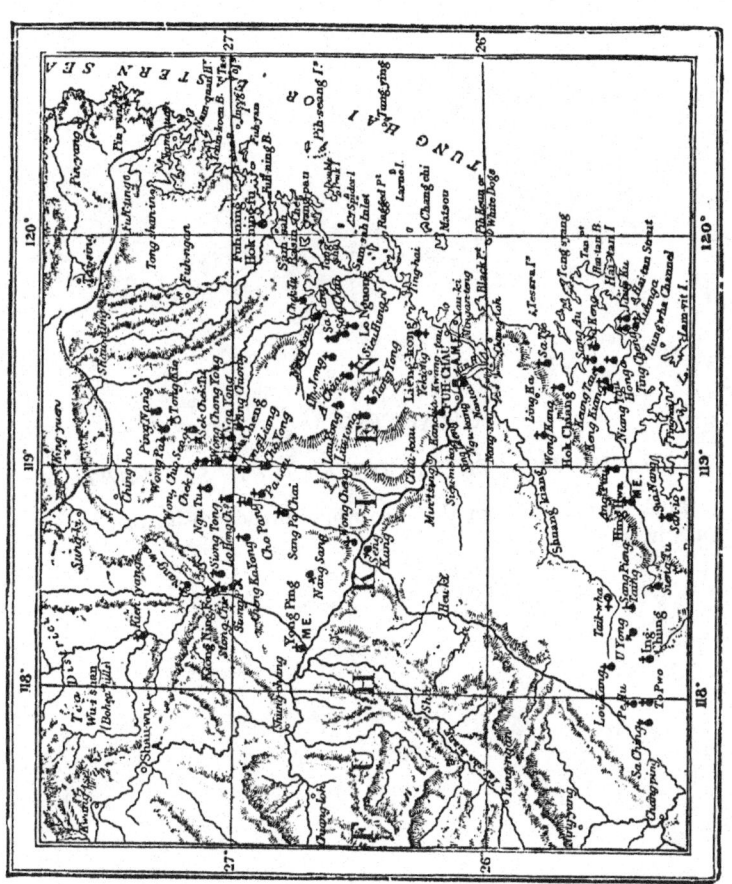

CHAPTER I

SOME REMINISCENCES OF ROBERT STEWART

"Look on the fields, for they are white already to harvest."—
JOHN iv. 35.

B

CHAPTER I

SOME REMINISCENCES OF ROBERT STEWART

(BY MR. EUGENE STOCK)

Lord, her watch Thy Church is keeping ;
   When shall earth Thy rule obey?
When shall end the night of weeping,
   When shall break the promised day ?
See the whitening harvest languish,
   Waiting still the labourers' toil ;
Was it vain—Thy Son's deep anguish?
   Shall the strong retain the spoil?

Tidings sent to every creature,
   Millions yet have never heard ;
Can they hear without a preacher?
   Lord Almighty, give the word.
Give the word ; in every nation
   Let the Gospel trumpet sound,
Witnessing a world's salvation,
   To the earth's remotest bound.

Then the end : Thy Church completed,
   All Thy chosen gathered in,
With their King in glory seated,
   Satan bound, and banished sin :
Gone for ever, parting, weeping,
   Hunger, sorrow, death, and pain ;—
Lo ! her watch Thy Church is keeping,
   Come, Lord Jesus, come to reign.

I HAD not known Robert Stewart well prior to
our going together to Australia, though I per-

fectly remember his ordination and departure for
China nineteen years ago.   But when the C.M.S.
Committee directed me to be their representative to
respond to the invitation that had come from the
Primate of Australia and other friends there, and I
was asked to name a clergyman and missionary to
accompany me, I gave Mr. Wigram three names, of
which Stewart's was one.   "Well, which of the three
shall I ask first?"   "Ask Stewart," I replied; for
there were only a few days left before we were to
sail, and I was sure of this, that he was a man ready
to go anywhere at a moment's notice in the service
of the King.   Next day came his answer from Bedford, "Yes"; and a most kind letter followed from
Mrs. Stewart, expressing her readiness that he should
go.   On March 18, 1892, we sailed in the P. and O.
s.s. *Britannia*.   Neither of us was strong.   Stewart
had suffered severely from dysentery in China, and
the doctors in England shook their heads about his
returning thither at all.   I was still very weak after
being prostrate for a month with influenza.   But the
voyage, through God's goodness, set us both up for
the work to which we were commissioned.

Stewart was the only clergyman on board (except
a young S.P.G. missionary for part of the way), and
he conducted the Sunday services.   These were all
that he considered it possible to arrange, except that
we had daily prayers in Holy Week, services on Good
Friday, and Holy Communion on Easter Day.   There
were scarcely any sympathisers with spiritual religion

on board, and no one cared to attend a Bible-reading;
but we two daily met for an hour at noon for reading, conversation, and prayer; and in a quiet way
Christian influence was exercised. Stewart's brightness and *bonhomie* made him popular with the
worldly men, and a very real affection was manifested to him by some. One, who was a leader in
the theatricals, sweepstakes, etc., seemed to feel a
personal sorrow because Stewart did not attend when
a couple of farces were acted; but to his question,
"My *dear* fellow, *why* didn't you come?" the un-
answerable answer was returned in another question,
"My *dear* fellow, why didn't you come to my service
on Sunday?" On the last day of our long voyage,
one of the chief officers came to me and said, "I
don't think your friend Mr. Stewart has the least
idea how the whole ship admires him. He has quite
altered my opinion of parsons. We've had a good
many at different times, but either they were so
stuck up one could not speak to them, or else their
talk in the smoking-room was worse than that of the
fast men; but Mr. Stewart is always pleasant, and
yet we all know what he's driving at "—which was,
that other men might know the happiness he had
himself found in the Lord's service. (Of course I in
no way endorse this officer's opinion of "parsons"; I
only record what he said.) Of more private work
on that and subsequent voyages, of souls striven for
and prayed for and won, I will not write; I am sure
Stewart would prefer that I made no allusion to them.

It was not by *resting* that he regained health in Australia ! In less than seven months we took more than three hundred meetings and services; and Stewart took quite half the speaking, and more than half the knocking about. In Victoria especially, he went long and untiring journeys by slow trains, or on rough roads, to address small gatherings in remote towns, while I was chiefly occupied at cities like Melbourne and Ballarat. His indomitable energy, his never-failing unselfishness, his humility and simple dependence on God, the earnestness and simplicity of his addresses, accomplished great things; and wherever he went, he won the love of all who came in contact with him. I have mentioned worldly men; let me also mention children. They all clung to him. One little boy, a clergyman's son, declared that he "should pray for Mr. Stewart every night," and began by doing so regularly; but one night, being very tired after an excursion, the little fellow got into bed too quickly—when his little sister ran up to him and tried to pull him out, crying "Oh you naughty boy : you've forgotten to pray for Mr. Stewart !" Let me parenthetically acknowledge that when Stewart afterwards told this story at a meeting in my hearing, he modified it by saying that the boy was to pray "for China." It was an excusable mis-statement !—but I happen to know that my version is the correct one.

Stewart's speeches were often very moving. Again and again I know of hearts very deeply touched by

his words on "I am a debtor," a subject he took re-
peatedly; and I am sure some Sydney friends must
remember his stirring address on "Now I know that
thou fearest God, seeing thou hast not withheld thy
son, thine only son." But he never had a thought of
"making a good sermon or speech." He aimed at
definite results. We used whenever possible to get
five minutes to pray together alone before going to
a meeting; and his prayer often was this, "Lord, if
Thou hast a message for any one whom Thou art
bringing to this meeting, give us that message to
deliver." Naturally, therefore, he believed in prayer
for a speaker as a real thing. I remember that at a
meeting at Bendigo, I was quietly writing letters
to England on my lap while he was speaking, as they
had to be posted that night. After the meeting he
gave me a gentle reproach: "While *you* were speaking, *I* was *praying*." I never wrote letters during
his speeches again! But while he was intensely
spiritual in his whole view of a missionary meeting,
he was intensely practical too. It was he who
pushed the Gleaners' Union, inviting people to come
to the platform then and there and be enrolled; which
procedure has done more than anything else to per-
petuate the missionary spirit in the Australian
parishes. He sold hundreds of Mr. Horsburgh's
booklet, *Do Not Say*; he distributed, only to *applicants*,
thousands of the C.M.S. Cycle of Prayer; he got
missionary boxes made, and placed more than a
thousand of them out himself—in this also doing a

work which has lasted, and has been most fruitful. These boxes he had labelled "New South Wales" or "Victoria" C.M. Association; but when we went to New Zealand, there was no Association there, nor did we know whether there could be one. Nevertheless, no sooner had his more cautious colleague left him at Auckland and gone on to Gisborne, than he got some scores of boxes made quickly, and put a label on them, "New Zealand C.M. Association"; and when we met again at Napier, and I shook my head at this pre-matureness, he only said, "Well, you see there *must* be an Association *now*!" And so there was presently; but not until he had already distributed most of his boxes.

I will venture to give one instance of his readiness to sink everything—even reputation with those whose good opinion he would most desire—if only he could get an undistracted hearing for his message. Some may think he did wrong on this occasion; I offer no opinion; but I honour his motive, and I think God used the opportunity. At one church, where he was to preach, he took his surplice, scarf, and hood out of his bag in the vestry, and was suddenly startled by the Incumbent's exclamation on seeing the plain black scarf: "Whatever is that thing?" "That? It's only my scarf." "Oh, you can't wear that: the congregation would stare at it all the time, and wonder what it meant." "All right," said Stewart; "I don't mind; I'll preach without one." "Oh, that will never do: look here, you had better wear ·

this one, and then people won't see anything unusual, and will listen to what you say." And with these words the Incumbent produced an embroidered white silk stole. "I had never worn such a thing before," said Stewart to me afterwards, "and I didn't like it; but I thought, never mind what I like—I want to get the people's ears—so I put it on." I will only add that to this day there are people who were in that church that morning, and received a message from God into their hearts then and there.

Of course one object before him in all his sermons and speeches was to set forth the Lord's claim upon His people for their personal service. Missionary meetings, he thought, should produce missionaries. Some of the Australasian men and women who have gone out lately into the mission field were the direct fruit of his addresses. His very first sermon, on the evening of the very day we landed at Melbourne, elicited the offer of those two dear sisters Saunders who afterwards joined him in China and laid down their lives with him. In England and Ireland, also, as many readers of this book know, he and Mrs. Stewart were especially used to call forth offers of service, and it was mainly through their influence that the noble band of women went to Fuh-kien in connection with the Church of England Zenana Missionary Society. Mrs. Stewart, indeed, was even more powerful as a speaker than her husband. I have been with her at a drawing-room meeting, appointed to speak after her, and when she sat down,

I have felt that any other address would only mar the effect of her loving, moving, burning words; and I have risen and simply said, " I will not add a syllable; let us pray over what we have heard."

Robert Stewart firmly believed that when the Lord Christ told His people to go into all the world, and to every creature, He meant what He said. Why should dangers or trials be considered? African mangrove-swamps might be deadly—Chinese mobs might be merciless; but how could such things affect our plain duty? Often did we talk of these matters; and often did he say, "One can only die once: what does it signify when or where? Let us do what God tells us, and let Him do what seemeth Him good." He was the very man to die at his post; and at his post he died. And Mrs. Stewart felt precisely the same. No one, after hearing one of her speeches, would have dared to put personal safety as the chief object of concern. As to the children, they were dedicated to China; and the more they saw of China in their earlier years the better—so, at least, felt their parents. Robert and Louisa Stewart were lovely and pleasant in their lives, and in death they were not divided.

The deep feeling aroused in Australia by the massacre is a significant token of the blessed influence that Stewart had exercised there. Melbourne, indeed, might naturally think especially of its own missionaries, Nellie and "Topsy" Saunders; but Sydney scarcely knew them, and yet from Sydney came the most touching expressions of love, and grief, and holy resolve to follow in the steps of Robert Stewart: memorial services in almost all the numerous churches, and in the cathedral; leading clergymen of a very different school from Stewart preaching sermons full of appreciation of him and his work; the dear honoured old Dean, in his eighty-eighth year, presiding over a crowded prayer-meeting three days after the news came, and bursting into tears as he gave out the opening hymn, "When I survey the wondrous cross." The letters I have received from men and women, young and old, who could not refrain from pouring out their hearts to Stewart's colleagues, are too personal to be quoted, but they all breathe the same spirit—not mere human sorrow, but sorrow mingled with joy, and with the strong expectation of rich blessing for Australia, and China, and the world, from those precious deaths. At Melbourne also there was a crowded special memorial service in the cathedral, Bishop Gre preaching most impressively; and although of course the world cavilled (as it did also at Sydney) at the wickedness of sending women to such a fate, the faith of the children of God was marvellously strengthened by the grace that shone forth from the bereaved widowed mother, Mrs. Saunders. If she had two more daughters, she told an "interviewing" press man, they should go for Christ to China; and she herself, writes Mrs. Macartney, would fain go to Ku-cheng and seek to win for her Lord some of the murderers, *and their children.*

So the Lord is going to do as He always does,

bring Life out of Death. Allen Gardiner's death by
starvation was the beginning of life for the Fuegians;
Livingstone's death in the heart of Africa brought
light into the Dark Continent; Hannington, murdered on the threshold of Uganda, purchased, as he
said, the road thither with his life; and God will
make the Ku-cheng massacre an event to look back
upon in eternity as the starting-point of a glorious
ingathering of souls. There is a triumph indeed in
store for those who can say, "Nothing too precious
for Jesus." "I believe," writes the father of Elsie
Marshall, one of the dear Stewarts' companions in
suffering, " that I shall see that glorious harvest in
China that is to spring up from those precious buried
grains that hold, in God's mysterious purpose, the
germs of eternal life; and I know I shall rejoice in
that day that God allowed me to call one of those
grains *mine*."

CHAPTER II
AMBASSADORS FOR CHRIST

CHAPTER II

AMBASSADORS FOR CHRIST

" Who are these who come among us
    Strangers to our speech and ways ?
Passing by our joys and treasures,
    Singing in the darkest days ?
Are they pilgrims journeying on
From a land we have not known ? "

" We are come from a far country,
    From a land beyond the sun ;
We are come from that great glory
    Round our God's eternal throne :
Thence we come and thither go ;
Here no resting place we know.

" Far within the depth of glory,
    In the Father's house above,
We have learnt His wondrous secret,
    We have learnt His heart of love :
We have seen and we have shared
That bright joy He hath prepared.

" We have seen the golden city
    Shining as the jasper stone ;
Heard the song that fills the heavens
    Of the Man upon the throne ;
Well that glorious One we know—
He hath sent us here below.

15

" We have drunk the living waters,
   On the Tree of Life have fed ;
Therefore deathless do we journey
   Midst the dying and the dead ;
And unthirsting do we stand
Here amidst the barren sand.

" Round us, as a cloud of glory
   Lighting up the midnight road,
Falls the light from that bright city,
   Showing us where He has trod ;
All that here might please the sight
Lost in that eternal light."

" Wherefore are ye come amongst us
   From the glory to the gloom ? "
" Christ in glory breathed within us
   Life, *His* Life, and bid us come.
Here as living springs to be—
Fountains of that life are we.

" Fountains of the life that floweth
   Ever downwards from the throne,
Witnesses of that bright glory
   Where, rejected, He is gone,
Sent to give the blind their sight,
Turn the darkness into light.

" There, amidst the joy eternal,
   Is the Man who went above,
Bearing marks of all the hatred
   Of the world He sought in love.
He has sent us here to tell
Of His love unchangeable.

" He hath sent us, that in sorrow,
   In rejection, toil and loss,
We may learn the wondrous sweetness,
   Learn the mystery of His cross—
Learn the depth of love that traced
That blest path across the waste.

" He hath sent us highest honours
   Of His cross and shame to win,
Bear His light through deepest darkness,
   Walk in white 'midst foulest sin ;
Sing amidst the wintry gloom,
Sing the blessed songs of home.

" From the dark and troubled waters
   Many a pearl to Him we bear ;
Golden sheaves we bring with singing,
   Fulness of His joy we share ;
And our pilgrim journey o'er,
Praise with Him for evermore."

                        T. P.[1]

VARIOUS proposals have been made as to writing a Life of Robert and Louisa Stewart ; but they have all been declined.

Lives so truly lived in secret with God are not easy to record. And even if the attempt were successfully made, is there not a danger of exalting the human and losing sight of the fact that " all things are of God ? "

It has been thought, therefore, that it is sufficient for God's glory, to print some letters lately received, and supply a few details of the earlier times. Their letters were not kept, at Mr. Stewart's earnest request.

Feeling that anything too personal would have been repugnant to the feelings of our dear brother and sister, we refrain from writing their biographies ; but we know their wish would be that we should write and print anything that would awaken love and sympathy for China and the Chinese—anything that would show the friends who have helped through prayer and by

---

[1] In " Hymns of Tersteegen, Suso and others," by Mrs. Bevan.

c

their gifts that the need now is not less, but greater. Their voices seem to plead with us from the glory, "Fill up the ranks." Who will be baptized for the dead?

They went out to Foochow in September, 1876, just after their marriage.

Learning the language was of course the first work.

Then Mr. Stewart was given charge of the school for native catechists belonging to the Church Missionary Society.

Mrs. Stewart, after a time, opened a school to train native Bible-women.

The money to build it was given by personal friends.

Then came the pressing need of English ladies to teach and superintend their Chinese sisters.

After eight years abroad Mr. and Mrs. Stewart came home, and the matter was taken up by the C.E.Z.M.S., who agreed to send ladies to China, arranging that the funds for India and China should be kept separate.

The all-absorbing thought was, "How can the Gospel be preached to this generation of the Chinese?" And visions rose of devoted English ladies residing in every one of the many cities of the Fuhkien province, superintending hundreds of native Bible-women.

These Bible-women cost £6 a year only, travelling expenses included. What a good investment of £6!

Dear readers, you who cannot go to China can have a substitute there for this modest sum; and I know not how many you may have "from the land of Sinim" to welcome you to "everlasting habitations."

Those who met Louisa Stewart at this time will remember the intense interest she felt and communicated to others on this subject of women's work (English and Chinese) in China.

How often she told, with glowing face, of her beloved Chinese women in the school! How at noon each day their lessons were suspended and a prayer-meeting held. So real and earnest were the petitions that the difficulty often was to stop them in time for dinner. They "believed in the Holy Ghost."

The history of one of these women, often told by Mrs. Stewart, was as follows :—

Mr. Stewart had received her husband, Ing Soi, into the C.M.S. school, and he asked that his wife might be under Mrs. Stewart's care to learn "the doctrine," so as to be able to help him when he was sent forth to teach.

Ing Soi was a man of God. Robert Stewart said he loved him as a brother. But the wife, though a Christian in name, showed no sign of true conversion to God. Alas! as her subsequent history shows, she was like many in our own country, who "will not come" at the voice of love, and must experience the goad of trouble, which "it is hard to kick against."

Mrs. Ing Soi wept over the difficult Chinese characters, and said it was impossible for her to learn to read; in fact, she did not care to read the book for whose Author she had no love; but, as the story will tell, at a day not very far distant her greatest desire was to search for herself the written Word, that she might find the living Word of God.

The time having arrived for her husband to go forth, she left the school.

It *seemed* as if no seed had been sown, and as if prayer were left unanswered. We *know* that every prayer is answered, though we may not at once *see* the answer. " Through faith and patience " we " inherit the promises."

After some time of happy work in the far-off city, Ing Soi went to see some converts in another town. They had hitherto visited him, but now they begged for a visit from their teacher.

One day he went. I believe it was a day's journey.

A manifesto from the mandarin greeted his eyes soon after his arrival. The walls were placarded with a notice forbidding any one to teach " the Jesus doctrine," and threatening confiscation of property, and possibly loss of life, to any one teaching " in this Name."

The ostensible reasons for these threats were an outbreak of cholera disease among the cattle, and failure in the crops—disasters usual in China in the fall of the year, but this year utilised by the Chinese authorities as a pretext for persecuting the Christians.

As Ing Soi read, he found himself seized by some men, who, holding his pigtail, said,—

" Do you promise not to speak any more in this Name ? "

"No," he answered firmly; "I will preach the Name of Jesus while I have breath. I live only to serve Him."

"Well, we must kill you."

They dragged him off to an opium den, where they beat him cruelly, and, putting a knife to his throat, threatened instant death unless he recanted.

"How did you feel, Ing Soi, when you faced death?" questioned Mrs. Stewart, to whom he recounted this experience after he reached Foochow.

"Oh!" he said—and his face, like Stephen's, shone as an angel's—"I never thought of death; my only thought was, in one moment I shall really *see* Jesus, and I was so full of joy they thought I was laughing, for they said, 'You needn't laugh; we are really going to kill you.'"

Just then the Mandarin interfered, lest matters should go too far, and with some vague dread of the English government.

With difficulty Ing Soi reached Foochow. He came to die; the injuries he had received were so serious.

For six weeks he lingered in the hospital, lovingly nursed by his wife, and visited daily by Mr. and Mrs. Stewart—not, as they said, for his sake alone; they found it good to be with him in the land of Beulah, and hear him speak the language of that country.

"Have you any fear of death, Ing Soi? Tell me," questioned Mr. Stewart one day.

"Living is death, dying is life," was the answer.

On another occasion he addressed his dearly-loved teacher,—

" One thing you will promise ? "

" That your wife and children may be cared for ? "

" Oh no! I know you will do all for them. I trust you and God, and I have no fear for them."

" What then ? "

" Those poor people who injured me. God has forgiven them. They did it in ignorance. I have asked the Lord to send them a teacher, and I want you to promise that if there is any inquiry you will not let any one punish them."

The promise was given. The likeness to Stephen was brought again to mind, and, indeed, to a greater than Stephen, who prayed, " Father, forgive them."

Ing Soi fell asleep in the arms of Jesus; but the story does not end here.

The seeds in the wife's heart now began to bring forth fruit.

The Christ-like spirit in her husband had been to her as the early and the latter rain, and she now begged her dear " sing-ang-iong " (teacher) to take her again into the school. God had put into her heart a great longing to be the messenger of mercy and forgiveness to her husband's murderers.

He fulfils " the desire of them that fear Him," and after her time of training she went—a real Bible-woman this time—to reap a harvest in other souls.

So it ever is: the seed is planted, and it grows, we " know not how," and brings forth " first the blade, then the ear, then the full corn in the ear" (is this the advancing manifestation in John xiv. 16, 21, 23—the Spirit, the Son, the Father?), and after that a harvest in other souls. Oh! is it not worth dying to all of the old self-life that we may "share in the glory of the harvest home"?

But we must return to the school with its twenty inmates.

In this unique boarding school for married women, some of them learning lessons with baby in arms, because baby could not be left behind, Mrs. Stewart spent some hours of every day.

Many of these women, with true heroism known to God alone, had walked weary miles with their " poor little feet," as they called them.

How Mrs. Stewart delighted, when she could find a ready listener, to tell of these dear pupils in China !

Sometimes they made her laugh in winter when it was cold (as it mercifully is in Foochow).

Chinese people think English fires very uncivilized, so destructive to furniture, and so apt to smoke. Their way of getting warm is to add jacket over jacket, and skirt over skirt; and when sitting quiet to embrace a little charcoal burner, hidden by the wide sleeves of the tunic.

Let us imagine Mrs. Stewart surrounded by her class of loving women. Some one gets specially interested, and forgets her unseen warm friend. Suddenly there is a cry that somebody is on fire! All hands haste to the rescue. The fire is put out without much injury, and a hearty laugh succeeds the momentary fear.

One day, early in the school experience, the teacher said in familiar sisterly converse: "You know now that the things said about us—such as that blue eyes see through the ground, and, that you would get harm if you came here—are not true. I am sure that some of the things said about you are not true. For instance, about killing the girl-babies. I do not suppose any of you have done so."

A smile passed from one to the other. Eighteen women out of the twenty present confessed to the crime, explaining that it had to be done immediately, before the little one had won any love! Poor babies—yet happy too. Here again Satan is vanquished. He suggests these cruel acts, but He who was manifested for this purpose, that He might destroy the works of the devil, destroys his power here, for death becomes life to these Chinese baby-girls. God has chosen the weak and despised things, and we praise Him for that third of the human race who die in infancy, saved through the blood of the Lamb.

In one letter Mrs. Stewart wrote (I quote from memory, not having kept the letter):—

"I am glad I believe in the Holy Ghost. Some of the women seem so hopelessly ignorant and stupid. They are brought up to believe that they have no souls, no minds, and that men only can think.

"One woman seemed unable to learn: she wept

over the characters. But quite suddenly she brightened up and learned quickly and well. I asked how it was.

"'Did you not tell us that God gives the Holy Spirit to those that ask?'

"'Yes.'

"'And that when He comes, He shall teach all things?'

"'Yes.'

"'That is how I learn now. He teaches me, and I cannot forget.'"

One more conversation repeated to us comes to mind. The women were explaining to Mrs. Stewart why marriage, as a rule, is regarded with dread by Chinese women; how they become drudges to the mother-in-law, and slaves, if not beasts of burden, to the husband; so that some young women have committed suicide rather than live to be taken to the husband's home.

Exclamations of surprise, if not of incredulity, arose when Mrs. Stewart said that in England girls who are engaged *like* to be married.

"Poor Chinese women," she would often say, "if friends at home could only see their hopeless faces, and know of their dark existence, they would indeed do *all* that they could for the women of China."

The woman—first in the transgression—God told of sorrow and of being under the rule of man.

The woman—mother of Jesus—last at His cross, first at His tomb. She died indeed to all natural goodness, but in Christ has she not been made alive?

As she has borne the image of the earthy, shall she not bear the image of the heavenly? Yes, truly. And as she was used of God in Christ's first advent, she has assuredly her part to fill up before the manifestation of the sons of God.

And when they come, the daughters as well as the sons, from the East and West, the North and South, the sacred Book adds: " And these from the land of Sinim."

"How can you say 'poor missionaries'? said Mr. Stewart in a sermon preached when he was last at home. " I tell you it is a life the highest archangel in heaven might envy."

The touching incidents connected with the leave-taking on their return to China in November, 1884, must be passed over; they both shrank from any personal publicity. They loved to make known far and wide what God had wrought.

To the glory of His grace, one remark must be repeated. Mrs. Stewart said to a relative of hers, " No one seems to understand but Mr. Hudson Taylor. Every one else says, ' When *must* you go back to China?'" (they were leaving three dearly loved children behind them); "but he said, ' When *can* you go back to China?' He understands."

And when that leave-taking was over, and a sister and some friends saw them off at Gravesend, the faces of both showed signs of passing through deep waters, but the light shining in the eyes of both also said, louder than any words, that He was with them. As they said themselves, they *loved* to go to China.

Time would fail to tell of sowing in tears and reaping in joy for two years more; and then again they came home, across Canada this time, because of Mr. Stewart's health.

He fought bravely on as long as the doctor would allow him to stay. First a change to Japan was tried.

There one night—his wife told of it afterwards—he lay insensible. They had gone high up in the mountains, to seek for him invigorating air.

Even the Japanese servants did not sleep in the inn; she was alone—alone with God. I believe that night she became Israel—not Jacob any longer. God became in a deeper sense all in all to her, and she had no fear, even face to face with the possibility that her husband might that night enter within the veil, without another word to her. She thought of the little children in China, the three boys at home, her mother and others in Ireland; and, looking her unknown future in the face, she praised God, telling Him she loved His will whatever it might bring to her. And a marvellous calm came over her whole being, and a joy not of earth !

Her husband was restored to her that time; but it was God's purpose to have him once more in England, and so He permitted the little strength he had gained in Japan to wane again.

Once more they turned homewards—a wonderful journey, as they afterwards said !

Every little detail so lovingly and graciously ordered ! The Lord carried His beloved child in His arms halfway round the world, when, humanly speaking, it seemed as if he could not reach home alive.

At first Mr. Stewart had to keep very quiet, but as soon as it was possible he was again in harness, preaching and holding meetings in the interest of his beloved China—or rather, of his beloved Lord. He was, indeed, a true follower of Him whose meat it was to do His Father's will.

The children, too, had a blessed training. Loving their father, and appreciating his society in a very special way, they were also taught to rejoice in the suffering entailed by his absence, because it was " for China."

In 1893 Mr. and Mrs. Stewart had again the joy of setting off for China, and what was really a joy too (though, perhaps, understood by few), of sacrificing natural inclination that they might embrace God's will.

A call came for missionary meetings in Canada. Who could be more suitable than Mr. and Mrs. Stewart—he to plead the cause of Christ, as he had done in Australia, New Zealand, and elsewhere; she to call upon her sisters in Canada to hear the cry of crushed womanhood in China ?

Again the choice to suffer was put before them. They had faced the good-bye to the three boys, now at a public school ; but what about the four wee ones— two little girls and two baby-boys? They could not be taken about Canada with their nurse on deputation.

No ; they must take the other way, and go by the

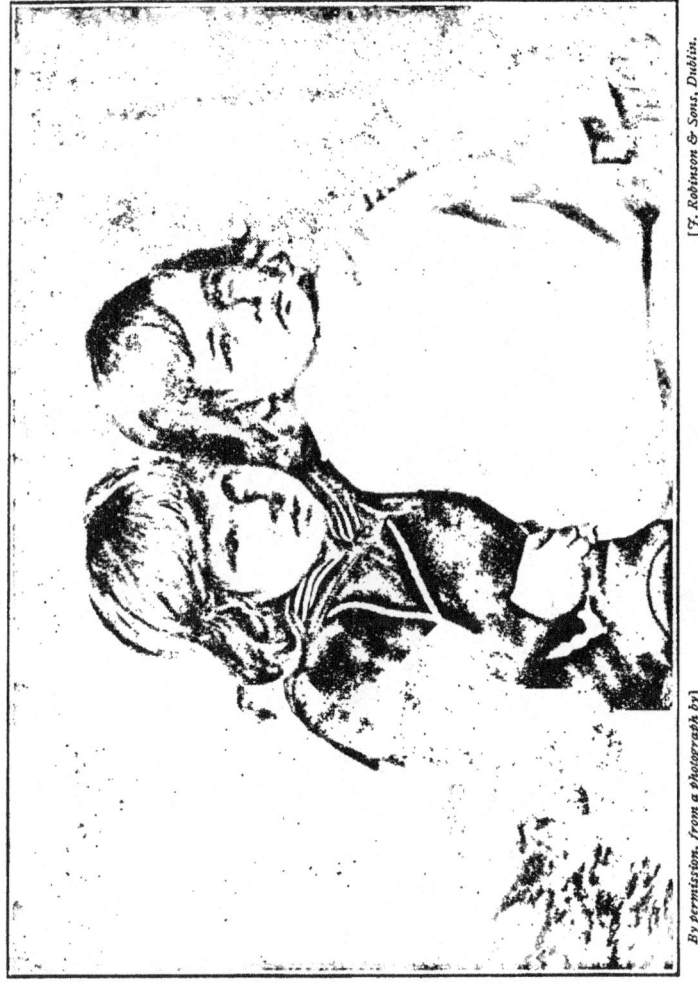

Herbert and Evan Stewart—the elder, Herbert, aged 6, was killed.

Red Sea, in company with some of the dear sisters going out under the C.E.Z.M.S., all of whom were ever cherished as dear sisters, if not daughters.

So it was decided, not grudgingly or of necessity. God loves a cheerful giver.

Dear Robert Stewart! If I have mentioned his wife —my sister—more, it is because we heard her *speak* more, not in any degree that we think less of him. Oh, no. Good soldier of Jesus Christ, patient, true servant, he never sought the praise of man, and always shrank from any recognition of his services ; he pitied those who sought such things. " Verily, they have their reward."

But he, seeing the invisible, and intensely devoted to the Captain of his salvation, ever pressed on, an inspiration to those who came in contact with him, and an example to all who would work while it is day.

From the Sunday morning when he, a young barrister, worldly and full of ambition, as some of us remember him, turned into Holy Trinity Church, Richmond, saying to himself that he knew his mother (then in glory) would be better pleased to see him there than boating on the Thames, as had been his intention when he left the house that morning—from that day until the fiery chariot parted us asunder on August 1, 1895, his course was "straight upward and straight onward to yonder throne." An old friend, alluding to his conversion, remarked, " I never saw a man so completely changed."

Dear Robert Stewart! we shall never see just such

another; but what thou wert God made thee, and to Him we give all the glory, as thou wert ever wont to do.

We must leave others to tell of work in Canada, and hasten to conclude this sketch. Christmas Day, 1893, witnessed a happy re-union of the four little ones, Lena the faithful nurse, the beloved parents, and some of the "sisters," whose love in the Spirit had been always a brightness in the Chinese life.

This time they passed through Foochow and went on to Kucheng—another answer to prayer, as their hearts were ever going out to the regions beyond. The name of Hwasang, which has now become sadly familiar to many ears, was first heard of as a sana-torium, where in the hottest part of summer they retreated with the children for refreshment and rest —rest, not only after work, but as a preparation for a fresh campaign.

There on the mountain top the native cottage stood which they bought for themselves.

During the summer of 1894 (last year) the letters from Hwasang were full of descriptions of peaceful rest, tea-picnics with the children, and other delights. In the month of June a new baby had come to gladden the home; they called her Hilda Sylvia. The little life of thirteen months was a bright one; she lived surrounded with love.

It is now known to all Christian friends the wide world over how Mr. and Mrs. Stewart passed through the golden gates together, followed by Herbert and the baby girl a little later.

I remember one day Mr. and Mrs. Stewart were at home, and some of us had gathered, a little family party, by the seaside in Wales. Herbert had had a fall, and might have been seriously hurt.

He said solemnly to his mother afterwards, " God went out to walk with Her to-day, or he would have been killed."

He was only two years old and called himself " Her," as Herbert was too long.

When I heard what had happened on August 1 and the succeeding days, I remembered his baby words, and I knew that "God walked with Herbert" then too, and with his father and mother, the baby sister, and the faithful nurse Lena. They were not " killed," they were translated. Had He not *promised* He would never leave them nor forsake them ?

" Some were tortured, not accepting deliverance, that they might obtain a better resurrection."

" Of whom the world was not worthy."

D

CHAPTER III

THE WHIRLWIND

CHAPTER III

THE WHIRLWIND

"And it came to pass, when the Lord would take up Elijah into heaven by a whirlwind, that Elijah went with Elisha. . . .

"And, behold, there appeared a chariot of fire, and horses of fire, and parted them both asunder ; and Elijah went up by a whirlwind into heaven."

" Thou sweet beloved will of God,
    My anchor ground, my fortress hill,
My spirit's silent, fair abode,
    In Thee I hide me, and am still.

Oh, will that willest good alone,
    Lead Thou the way, Thou guidest best ;
A little child, I follow on,
    And, trusting, lean upon Thy breast.

Thy beautiful sweet will, my God,
    Holds fast in its sublime embrace
My captive will, a gladsome bird,
    Prisoned in such a realm of grace.

Within this place of certain good
    Love evermore expands her wings ;
Or, nestling in Thy perfect choice,
    Abides content with what it brings.

Oh, lightest burden, sweetest yoke !
    It lifts, it bears, my happy soul,
It giveth wings to this poor heart ;
    My freedom is Thy grand control.

Upon God's will I lay me down,
　　As child upon its mother's breast ;
No silken couch, nor softest bed,
　　Could ever give me such deep rest.

Thy wonderful grand will, my God,
　　With triumph now I make it mine,
And faith shall cry a joyous Yes !
　　To every dear command of Thine."

THE storm that burst on August 1, 1895, at
Hwasang (the summer resort of our dear
missionaries) was not altogether without warning.

The following letters tell their own tale. Mrs.
Stewart's letter, written as early as December 10,
1894, shows that already there was earnest need for
prayer. Her journal letter, and Mr. Stewart's letter,
written to the Church Missionary Society a little
later, show how surely, though slowly, the clouds
were gathering.

But later letters—some extracts from which are
given towards the end of this chapter—give us
pictures of our friends enjoying their quiet rest at
Hwasang, and looking forward with joyful hope
and confident expectation to their "Keswick Week,"
which they kept at the same time as the great gathering by Derwentwater.

The following letter from Mrs. Stewart, dated
December 16, 1894, addressed to Mrs. Baldwin, for-
merly at Foochow in connection with the American
Mission, was inserted in the letter leaflet of the
Women's Auxiliary :—

" MY DEAR MRS. BALDWIN,—

"Your kind suggestion that I should send you now and then topics for special prayer has been in my mind much to-day, and I feel that I must write and tell you of our great need. You will, of course, have guessed that owing to the war between China and Japan, Chinese people are in a state of great unrest, and hardly know what to expect from day to day. In this part of the Fuh-kien Province a new source of danger has arisen. A secret society, which has been slowly growing for two years, has suddenly become very active, and is rapidly increasing in numbers; some hundreds have joined them within the last few weeks, and they are daily growing in numbers. The Mandarin has no power to check them; he made an attempt a few weeks ago, and his house was soon surrounded by an angry mob, who said they would pull it down if he did not agree to all their wishes. At last the poor man yielded, as he was quite terrified, and actually allowed his own secretary to be beaten, merely because the mob demanded it, and then liberated a few of their number he had imprisoned, and sent them home in state in sedan chairs. The victory over the Mandarin has made them very bold, and they say quite openly they can now do as they like. They have many times threatened to burn down our houses, and either kill us or drive us away; but the Lord has kept us in perfect peace; we realize fully that we are safe in His keeping, for we have no human power to trust

to. The Mandarin can no longer help himself, so
there is no protection from him, and the officials at
Foochow are powerless: such consternation prevails
owing to the Japanese victories. But we know nothing
can hurt us without our Father's will, and we feel quite
content. Our little girls, aged ten and twelve, sometimes feel the strain rather, and when people begin
talking of possibilities they feel rather frightened;
but even this the Lord is using for good, for it is
teaching them to turn to Him for help and comfort, as
they never would in peaceful days. We feel most for
our poor Christians, and it is for them I want specially
to ask you to pray. Even now many are having a
time of severe testing, and much worse may come if
the war is prolonged. The heathen think they have
now a good chance of injuring them, as the Government is quite unable to take their part at present.
Some have had their crops of rice cut down and
carried away before their eyes; others have been
beaten; and one poor man had his shop attacked, and
everything he had carried off. We know that those
who are grounded and settled in the faith will not be
moved, but we feel so much for the inquirers, and
those just lately come out of heathen darkness. 'God
is able to make them stand.' Will you join with us
in asking that all this trouble may lead to great
spiritual blessing, and that the Christians may be
given courage to bear whatever may be the Lord's
will to send them? Will you also pray that this
secret society, which is doing so much harm, may be

in some way broken up, and not allowed to injure the
Lord's work in this place? They are going to have
a great gathering of some hundreds of these con-
spirators at this city in about a fortnight, and we are
praying much that the Lord will keep them from
doing any harm. They threaten all sorts of things,
but we know they cannot carry them out unless God
permits them. The Consul is anxious we should all
leave these inland stations, and go down to the Treaty
Port for safety, for he thinks that if Pekin is taken
there may be a general rising of the people, and then
the 'foreigner' would be the first to suffer. But so
far we cannot see that it is the Lord's will we should
leave our posts, and we fear it would much discourage
the Christians if we did so. The Lord will guide day
by day, and we want simply to follow His will. Will
you pray specially for two dear men, leaders in the
Church here at Kucheng? The first is named Ling
Sing-mi; he is an ordained clergyman, the pastor of
our church in the city, and head of the Kucheng
district work under my husband. Will you pray that
he may be given wisdom and strength at this time of
trial, that God may bless him, that he may be a
blessing to others? The other is a man named
Li Daik-in, also a leader, and also a very good man.
Will you ask that he too may receive much blessing
through this trial, and learn to trust God more fully
than ever before? We are all well in health, thank
God. My husband has had one attack of illness since
the summer, but is now well again; he is constantly

busy, and, indeed, can hardly get through the work of these two great districts. Will you ask the Lord to send more men—men fitted and prepared by Himself? Our warmest thanks for your sympathy in our work."

The following letters, written in April, 1895, by Robert Stewart, show that all needful precautions were taken. They knew the angels had charge to "keep them in *all* their ways," but they were not rashly tempting God.

"Reuter's Agency is informed that the district referred to in the Hongkong telegram as 'nearer Foochow than Kucheng,' contains several Church Missionary Society stations, Church of England Zenana stations, and American Methodist stations. The most important of these are Fukhieu, Fuhning, Longuong, Ningtaik, all to the north of Foochow, and Hokchiang, and Hinghwa, to the south of that city. At some of these stations there are male missionaries, and ladies at most of them. The following letter—the last one received—from the Rev. R. W. Stewart, addressed to the Church Missionary Society, and communicated by them to Reuter's Agency, is dated Kucheng, April 8, and shows that even then the situation was critical.

"Mr. Stewart says:—

"'We have been having some rather exciting times here lately. Ten days ago I was called up at four o'clock in the morning by our native clergyman and

other Christians, who had crossed the river to our
house to bring the startling news that the Vegetarian
rebels were expected at daylight to storm Kucheng
and that the gateways of that city were being blocked
with timber and stone as fast as possible. We have
for a considerable time been aware that the Vegetarians were recruiting in large numbers, and the
expectation that something of this kind might happen
led the better-class people to subscribe large sums for
the rebuilding of the city wall, which in many places
had fallen down; the gates, too, had been either
broken or were gone. At the time when the alarm
was given, we had, with women, girls, and children,
nearly one hundred sleeping in our compound. The
rebels expected in an hour! What was to be done?
As we talked, and prayed, and planned, the dawn
began to break; then came the rain in torrents.
What part this played in the matter I don't know;
but as we saw it falling heavily, and remembered the
Chinese fear of getting wet, we said to one another,
"The rain will be our protection." At daylight we
roused the schools, and, after a hasty meal, all left
in a long, sad procession to make their way across
the river in a small ferry-boat, which came backwards and forwards for them, until at last the whole
party had reached the other side. It was a long
business, all in the rain, and then the wall had to be
climbed by a ladder, for by this time the blocking of
the gateways was complete. Near our chapel the
wall had not been rebuilt to its full height; and the

chapel ladder, the only one to be obtained, just reached
to the top. This was one of the many incidents that
showed us that the hand of God was controlling
everything. The next day that part of the wall was
built to its proper height, and the ladder would have
then been several feet too short, and we could never
have got the women with their cramped feet and the
children over the wall.

"'For the next three days the wall was guarded by
bands of citizens, posted at short intervals from one
another, and armed with the best weapons they could
find; but, indeed, they were poor things—old three-
pronged forks, centuries old, to judge by their appearance, with movable rings on the handles to
shake, and so strike terror to the hearts of the foe.
Rusty, too, were their swords, and rarely to be seen;
we watched the proud possessors washing them in a
pool and scraping them with a brick. The majority
had no scabbards; not that the "braves" had thrown
them away, but they had lost them. One I examined
had a useful sort of scabbard: it covered all but the
last couple of inches of the blade, so you could stick
your enemy without the bother of pulling it out—a
good thing if you were in a hurry. Those three days
whilst the city was straitly shut up were anxious
ones. Then the gates were opened. What took place
between the Mandarin and the Vegetarian leaders we
do not know; but no one believes that we have seen
the end of the matter. Such a serious affair cannot be
so easily patched up; probably we have as yet had

but the beginning. Much depends upon the course
that the war takes. If a treaty is arranged during the
present armistice of three weeks, I think perhaps all
will be quiet. Soldiers can be spared from Foochow,
and some arrests of the ringleaders can be effected,
and that will quell it; but if not, the rebels will have
recruited in sufficient numbers to make a rising a
success.

" 'Our girls' and women's schools have, of course,
been disbanded, and your ladies have left for Foochow, I need hardly say very sorely against their
will. It was hard for them to leave their loved work
and their many friends amongst the Chinese; but
they saw clearly it was best, for they could not help
them in the event of a disturbance, and might rather
hinder their flight and make concealment more difficult. Our Consul wrote, strongly urging this step
should be taken, and the American Consul wrote to
his people in the same strain; so the ladies have gone
very obediently, but very sadly, all of them wishing
they were men, and so not obliged to retreat. But I
think they see in all that is happening the finger of
God pointing to a cessation of their work for a time,
perhaps that they may leave Him to work alone.
When they come back, they may be astonished to find
the wonders that the Spirit of God has done in their
absence. The Japanese have taken Tamsui, on
Formosa, and are hovering about Foochow. I hope
they will not land. They have many well-wishers
among the Chinese. Here eight out of ten of the

lower and middle classes would rejoice at a Japanese
victory. They hate their own Government, and are
rebels at heart. It would take very little to make
them so in fact. But Hezekiah's God is ours. One
angel slew 185,000 men, so with the Lord of Hosts
of angels on our side there is nought to fear.' "

" The Rev. R. W. Stewart writes in a more recent
letter :—

" ' KUCHENG, *April* 21.

" ' As you know, all the ladies have been moved from
here to the coast, to see what the Japanese intend
doing. The general belief is that a treaty is about
to be agreed to; and if so, we need expect no more
trouble here of a serious kind. God holds the key of
the unknown. Your Lang-yong and Sa-yong ladies
have not moved; all in peace there. The others will
be back here soon, I expect.' "

And Hezekiah's God *was* true to them, as He ever
is, and must be to His children. For that time, the
storm passed by.

When all danger was supposed to be over, they
returned to Kucheng, and shortly afterwards went to
Hwasang, their summer resort, where, on August 1,
as already stated, the storm burst.

Though some things already told occur again in
this journal-letter of Mrs. Stewart, we put it in as
it is. Simply and naturally she writes to her own
friends, and as well as general information about the
" Vegetarians," it gives us a glimpse of the happy
family life, even when surrounded by danger.

She had learned that lesson, " In *everything* give
thanks ": even when her little girls were frightened
by the news of the " Vegetarians," because it taught
them " to turn to Him for help and comfort, as they
never would in peaceful days." She *saw* as well as
believed, that " *All* things work together for good to
them that love God."

Mrs. Stewart's Journal-Letter.

" *March* 27*th*, Evan's birthday.—We had a quiet,
peaceful day, with no indication of coming trouble.
The children had their tea out of doors as a birthday
treat, and the three sisters, who happened to be in
Kucheng, came and joined us. That night, about 12
o'clock, our two leading men, Mr. Sing-mi and Mr.
Daik-ing, came to our house to tell us the Mandarin
had men hard at work all night barricading the
gates; the walls were nearly finished, but no gates
put up; however, the Chinese are equal to any
emergency, and the old gates were quickly put in,
and huge strong boards they use for coffins nailed
behind, also great pieces of stone; so that, from
inside, the fortifications looked quite formidable. I
think all the coffin-shops in the city must have been
rifled! However, this was the startling news brought
to us in the middle of the night! What was to be
done? We had our 100 women and children sleeping
in our compound, between the women's and girls'
schools; besides, we had the lady missionaries and
all our own children. Clearly, we could not do

anything in the darkness. The road between us and
the city is steep and difficult, and there is a small
river to cross. Many plans were discussed, and much
time was spent just waiting upon God to know His
will. In a wonderful way His promise was fulfilled
to us, 'Thou wilt keep him in perfect peace whose
mind is stayed on Thee.' We felt so certain God was
guiding, that we could go on watching for each
indication of His will. Just as we were standing
talking together, heavy rain began to fall, and Mr.
Sing-mi said quietly, 'There is one answer to our
prayers. Even Vegetarians will do little on a day like
this!' Well, as soon as light came, the ku-niongs
(young ladies) were wakened up, and all the women
and girls. It was decided that all should move at
once over to the buildings adjoining our city Church,
as they were safer inside the walls than at our
houses, which stand outside. It took some time to
get them all started; and while I was looking after
them, and helping to get them off, Lena packed a few
necessary articles in a basket, as we felt our houses
would probably be the first attacked if the Vegetarians
really arrived. We had to make great speed, for all
the gates were by this time blocked up, and men were
busy building up the only place on the wall still
rather low. I forgot to say that the Mandarin had
sent over his card asking us all to go over to the
City, saying he could not give us any protection outside the walls. At last, the women and girls were
all safely housed in the city. There was a ladder

belonging to the Church, which was fortunately *just* long enough to reach the lowest part of the wall, and up this all had to climb. Then our own party started, the two little boys in baskets carried by our trusty coolie (a basket on each end of a bamboo stick), baby in Lena's arms, and the little girls with their father. I called for the three sisters on my way past the 'Olives,'—Hessie Newcombe, Miss Weller, and Miss Wade, who had been only just one week in Kucheng. At last the river was crossed, the ladder ascended, and the city entered, and we found ourselves at the house of one of the American missionaries, Mr. Wilcox, who was away at Foochow with his wife and family. Dr. Gregory, a medical missionary, was the only representative of the Mission, and, with his permission, we took possession of the empty house. In a short time we got all settled; we found beds enough and had brought bedding with us. We were glad we had lost no time in moving, for by the afternoon the wall at the place we got over was so high that, standing on the top rung, the person's hands could only touch the top of the wall, and they had to be pulled up by people standing on the top. The wall was guarded by people hired by the Mandarin for the purpose. We heard he was paying them $200 a day, as he had engaged 1,000 men. I can almost believe it, for we watched groups of men passing to and fro continually, on the look-out to give the alarm should the Vegetarians be seen approaching.

" Three days we spent in the city, the people all the

E

time grumbling because the gates were shut and they
could not get out to do their work in the fields or gather
brushwood on the hills to make fires to boil their rice.
At last placards were posted up all over the city, saying
that 'when the Mandarin oppresses the people rebel,'
and it was openly said that if the gates were not
opened they would force them open themselves; and
then, of course, would be the opportunity for the Vegetarians.   Accordingly they held a council of war, and
after much prayer it was decided that it was very important to get the children away at any rate; and that
of course led to my going, as baby could not be sent
without me.   Our chief native helpers strongly advised
sending all the women and girls away as soon as
possible to their own homes, as they thought they
would be much safer than anywhere near us; they
also thought it safer for the sisters not to visit just
then, while the people were in such an excited state.
It therefore seemed wiser, as there was no special
reason for staying, to divide, and to go to Foochow
for a time till things quieted down.   I need not say
how sad we felt to come to this conclusion; but it
made it almost impossible that any one should escape if
we all stayed, for chair coolies are never forthcoming
in times of great excitement, and Cui-kan, where we
take boat for Foochow is 30 miles from Kucheng!
So not many amongst us could walk it!   No sooner
said than done.   The packing at once began, chairs were
ordered, and after dinner we started.   We heard that
one gate was supposed to be opened that afternoon, so

the long procession proceeded along the top of the great wide wall, till near the gate we descended to the streets, only to find the gate barred and barricaded and no signs of opening whatever. We turned away hoping to find some friendly ladder by which to make our exit, and, to our joy, not very far away was one discovered, and for the sum of forty cents the man was bribed to allow us to use it. Robert got down first, but just as he reached the ground our friend of the ladder got some idea into his head, and decided we were not to go! To our horror, he began shouting and vociferating loudly, and trying to haul up the ladder; Robert held on to the lower part, and it seemed as if it was going to be a struggle as to which was the strongest. Robert, however, got two strong Chinamen to come to his aid by promise of a little money, and at last our sturdy ladder man yielded. Now we had time to observe that the ladder was all too short, indeed was about four feet short of the ground.

" There was nothing on which to prop it up, but Robert and his two assistants held it up in their hands till we had all safely reached the ground. The little ones first, then all the ku-niongs one by one. Robert came with us a short way from the wall, and then felt he ought to return, as he might have difficulty in getting back if he was late. It did seem hard to go on and leave him behind, but to stay there with the little ones and baby only meant additional peril to him.

" That night we only travelled six miles, and reached one of our chapels at a place called Co-tong. We got

there about dark, and our little washerman began
bustling about to get us some supper. The cook
stayed in the city with Robert, but the Chinese can be
'Jack of all trades,' so the washerman turns cook
when there is any need. After tea, the next thing
was to find beds for such a large party, but the
catechist was equal to the occasion, and produced a lot
of forms and bed-boards, which are all a Chinese bed
consists of; we had our own wadded quilts and blankets in our baskets. So we were soon all in bed.

"At daylight the coolies were all astir, and made such
a noise we could not go on sleeping; so we got up and
dressed, and then found our good little man had got
breakfast ready for us. We started in our chairs about
seven o'clock. Baby rode with me, Herbert and
Kathleen in a chair together, Mildred with Evan, Lena
in a chair to herself; and five ku-niongs made up our
procession. Cui-kan was reached about five o'clock.
A man who had been sent on before us got two
boats, so we went at once and took possession. They
were native boats with covering of matting. There
was a long delay about paying our chair coolies, and
waiting for some of our baskets that had not arrived,
and at last we began to feel very impatient to start.
However, as we found afterwards, these very delays
were being ordered by the Lord, and Robert was at
that very time praying in Kucheng that 'the wheels
of our chariots might be taken off!' Just as we were
persuading the boatman he ought really to push off, a
man rushed up and put a piece of paper into my hand;

it was a scrap written in great haste by Robert, saying
the Mandarin had made peace with the Vegetarians,
that the city gates were opened, and that we might
return safely; only he thought the children had better
go on with Lena to Foochow for a little time.

"We were indeed glad and thankful, but sorry for
the disappointment of the little ones, for they had so
looked forward to having us all with them; but I must
say they behaved beautifully. They *looked* a little sad
of course, but they never said one grumbling word,
and seemed trying to make it easy for me. We quickly
put all they would need in the smallest of the boats,
gave them their supper, and food enough for breakfast,
sent one of our two menservants with them, and saw
them off floating down the lovely river Min towards
Foochow. (I might say here they arrived next
morning about twelve o'clock, and were taken into the
'Olives' by kind Miss Stevens, who made them very
happy.)

"After their departure we proceeded to have our
own supper, and then prepared for the night. We
spread our wadded coverlets on the deck, all in a row,
and had a fairly good night. Baby rather disturbed
some of the party, I fear, but Hessie Newcombe exclaimed next morning, 'Oh, you little darling, you slept
all the night through!'—which showed us that Hessie
herself had, at any rate, slept well. Next morning
we started back. It rained the early part of the day,
so the coolies would not start, and we only got half
way by dusk. That night, therefore, we had to enjoy

the luxuries of a Chinese hotel. It is *not* a treat, I must confess. We were shown into a small, dark room, the walls of which were lined with the usual Chinese wooden beds. Just space enough was left in the middle for a square table, where we had our meals. Six of us, not including baby, had to sleep in the same room; or rather try to rest, for we did not sleep much.

"Next day we finished our journey to Kucheng, arriving about three o'clock. As our chairs passed the city, it was nice to see the gates open, but we noticed men were still working vigorously at the wall. Robert met us at the ferry, and poor little tired baby was glad to go to him and be carried to the house. Leu-luk, the Chinese girl who assists me, soon came to help, so I was able to begin to put the house in order, which was rather upset by our sudden flight. However, we found, soon after our arrival, that things were not going on as satisfactorily as had been at first expected. Rumours kept flying about of gatherings of Vegetarians at certain places, and all sorts of threats were used as to what they were going to do, to Christians and heathens alike who were possessed of any property. We had a prayer meeting at eight o'clock each morning with the Christians, which was a source of great comfort to us all. So a week passed away, and then our messenger arrived from Foochow, bringing letters. One was from our Consul, telling us that the Japanese had come south; that they had taken a port in Formosa (which afterwards turned out to be untrue); that they were threatening an

attack on Foochow; and that if they did so, and all
the Chinese soldiers should be detained at Foochow,
he felt sure that the Vegetarians would make the most
of the opportunity, and would very likely make an
attack on the foreigners because under the protection
of their Government. He therefore insisted on all the
ladies and children leaving the district. Again we
had to pack up, and again sorrowfully to leave our
beloved Kucheng. We journeyed, as before, to
Cui-kan, and sent on a trusty man to hire a boat for
us. When we reached the hill overlooking the river,
we waited to hear if a boat had been found, for, once
down in the streets, we get surrounded with crowds of
people. At last the man came back, saying there was
no boat to be had! that soldiers were being sent
down from cities higher up the river to help defend
Foochow, and every available boat was secured by
them. It seemed sad news. We could not go back
very well even one stage to look for an inn, our coolies
were so tired; and the inns are so bad in Cui-kan no
one likes to stay in them. It was getting dark too,
and cold, and poor little baby was coughing a good
deal, and I longed to find some shelter for her. I
could only tell the man to try again, and that he
might offer a little extra money as the case was
urgent. Again we prayed and waited, and again he
returned unsuccessful. At last he came back saying
he had found one boat that would take us if we would
be willing to share it with two soldiers and a horse!
He added, ' They will tie up the horse, so you need not

be afraid.' We gladly accepted, even though we had
to pay more than we usually do for a boat all to
ourselves. We were only too glad to get any shelter
for our heads, for by this time rain was beginning to
fall, and darkness fast approaching. This time there
was no friendly letter to stop us, and soon our boat
got off. We were all so tired that as soon as we could
get something to eat we lay down and tried to get
some sleep. I searched in vain for some sheltered
nook for baby; the wind seemed to whistle through
the frail covering of our boat, and, in spite of shawls
and rugs and a barricade of baskets, she caught a
heavy cold that is not well yet. Next day we reached
Foochow, but not till two o'clock, as the wind was
against us. We sent at once for native chairs, and
all our party, except myself, went off direct to the
' Olives,' the only house just then in Foochow that
had room for us. I was so anxious about Robert that
I decided I would go at once to see the Consul, and
tell him just how matters stood in Kucheng. Nellie
Saunders kindly took baby from me, and I knew Lena
would be at the ' Olives ' to receive her. The Consul
was most kind; said he was very glad we had come
down, for he felt a very great responsibility. He
added, ' I never like to disturb missionary work till it
is absolutely necessary.' . . .

"After a few days' rest we arranged that we would
take possession of the C.E.Z. summer resort up in the
hills near Foochow, and wait till the Lord should
open the way for us to return to Kucheng. We felt

led to this decision for several reasons ; one, that Foochow is very unhealthy this time of year, and it was better for the children and those studying the language to be away from it ; and also we are in Chinese dress, and we have at present no other. We are more convinced every day that the native dress is the best for the work. Even at Foochow we heard every one make favourable observations on us. 'How much nicer that dress is than the foreign!' is a very common remark; and some women call out, 'Do look! her petticoat is just like ours, and her jacket too ; her hair is done the same way, and her shoes *do* look nice. If it were not for the eyes, she would look *just* like us! And some even say these are the 'Cing-cing hunggau,' the true Christians. . . . I am writing now in the Kuliang 'Olives,' and have with me, besides the children, L. Wade, the two Saunders, Elsie Marshall, and Annie Gordon. . . . Robert writes that all is quiet at Kucheng, waiting to see how the war gets on. . . . He has arranged that all the Christians throughout our district shall meet together at 7 o'clock every morning to pray, trusting in God alone to protect them. We believe it will bring great blessing."

A very interesting letter appeared in *The Newcastle Daily Chronicle* of August 13, from Dr. W. P. Mears, dated Teignmouth Artillery Camp, Redcar. He writes from experience gained by some years' travel and residence in the disturbed district.

The following is an extract from his letter. He

describes not only the mutterings of the storm, as the
missionaries' own letters do, but the great whirlwind
that took them from our sight. . . .

" Knowing intimately, as I did, the late Rev. R.
Stewart, I am fully persuaded that he would be the
last man to do anything to excite the animosity of
any of the natives. When I reached China he had
been for some time invalided at home. Yet everywhere the people—not one or two, but scores—spoke
of him with a loving respect, and a most genuine
desire for his return. In Kucheng, round him he
had upwards of two thousand native Christians and
over 500 regular communicants, all these last being
men who had been well tested by at least two years'
probation. The Vegetarians dared not attack him
there. They waited till he had left the city, as he
would do at the beginning of August on account of
the heat, and had gone with the majority of the
Europeans to the little sanatorium of the Kucheng
missionaries, four hours' journey off, among the hills.
Hardly had he taken possession of one of the two or
three small bungalows there, where he and the others
were far remote from any assistance except that of a
few terrified villagers, when the assassins crept up in
the darkness, just before dawn, fired the house,
prodded their victims as they rushed out, and
promptly scattered, not waiting to complete their
devilish work, or to attack the other bungalows a few
hundred yards farther off, where the few foreigners
were already aroused. Mr. Stewart was in every

way a thorough man, whom to meet was to respect and love—a man without fear, and without fanaticism. Such men—men like Livingstone, Mackay of Uganda, and others—are the pioneers who clear the way for British influence, civilization, and religion, whose lives are examples to every man, whose deaths are losses to the nation."

His expression "devilish work," when speaking of the assassins, is not too strong.

"Thou couldest have no power at all against Me, except it were given thee from above," said Jesus.

This is equally true of every member of His body.

God could have sent legions of angels to deliver them, had that been His will; but when He would "take them up into heaven by a whirlwind, . . . behold, there appeared a chariot of fire, and horses of fire, and parted them asunder." Those who are left represent to us Elisha. God grant to them a double portion of His Holy Spirit! We pray Him to work miracles of grace through them, as He did through Elisha

The following extract is from a letter from Miss Codrington, dated Hwasang, July 20, 1893, received September 9:

"We are having a very happy, restful time up here. Mr. and Mrs. Stewart are looking less tired than they did; the girls and boys look well, the baby improving.

"Next week we hope to have our 'Keswick Meet-

ings,' and are believing and praying for much blessing."

How beautifully God arranges everything; their
last week on earth specially filled with waiting upon
Him in praise and prayer !

Miss Tolley's letter of an earlier date mentions the
other workers, and tells in the natural style of a
"home letter," how God chose those who were to
wear the martyr's crown and how others were
spared.

Has not God specially called these to blessed work
for Him ?   And we know He will fill their lives with
praise.

> "Not for the lips of praise alone, or e'en the praising heart I
> ask ;
> But for a life made up of praise in every part."

God asks us to let Him make us channels of blessing, through believing prayer, to those who have been
left behind.   Their names and special work will be
found in chapter iv., which is devoted to "Foreign
Women."

Here, let us record the names of our happy dead, or
rather of those who went from their "Keswick Week"
to join "the general assembly and church of the First-
born," and the "innumerable company of angels."

We too "are come" to that "city" (Heb. xii. 22);
and so these dear ones, whose names we give, have
not left us.   For are they not "in God," who "is not
far from any one of us"?

> ## "With Christ."
> Robert Warren Stewart.
> Louisa K. Stewart.
> Hessie Newcombe.
> Elsie Marshall.
> Flora Lucy Stewart.
> Mary Ann Christina Gordon.
> Harriette Elinor Saunders.
> Elizabeth Maud Saunders.
> Herbert Stewart (aged 5).
> Hilda Sylvia Stewart (1 year).
> Helena Yellop (the faithful nurse).

Left behind: Florence Codrington; Mildred, Kathleen and Evan Stewart, aged respectively, twelve, ten, and three.

Let us not forget Mrs. Stewart's request for prayer, for their dear native Christians, always so near their hearts.

Robert and Louisa Stewart knew no class distinction, they cherished no race prejudice.

They believed that "God has made of one blood all nations of men."

The following extracts from Miss Annie Tolley's journal-letter give us some bright homely glimpses of the C.E.Z.M.S. ladies, working and resting:

"*May* 15*th*.—Lucy went to Dangiong for me, to teach the women for me.   The Bible-woman went to Uongbah, for the class there, instead of Flora, and then Hessie read to Flora and me, while I lay on my bed.   We had a very nice afternoon.   You know I was not well from fever then.   The next day I went myself in a chair to Hokdong and took the class there, speaking on ' the pearl of great price.'   Flora and one of the girls from the station class went to Sengsang for the class there.

" The next day (Friday afternoon) Hessie and I spoke to the women at the Friday afternoon prayer meeting.   We had such a nice time.

" In the evening, there was the prayer meeting, when the catechists and all the men and boys gather together in our hall, we sitting with the women behind a red screen.

" *May* 21*st*, *Tuesday*.—Made medicine for a boy. Taught five children in school.   Read with teacher (studying Chinese), till a man came, saying Mr. Stewart was on his way to us.

" Flora and I got a room ready for him, and in the afternoon he arrived.

" We were delighted to see him, and we talked all about the doings in Kucheng, etc.   In the evening he took prayers for us, and saw the women in the school.[1]

" We went late to bed.

---

[1] The school is for training native Bible-women.

" The next day (*May 22nd*) it pelted with rain. After breakfast Mr. Stewart spoke to us on Isaiah ix. 1–7, and 1 Corinthians iii. 10–15, telling us that there are two ways of working: one the fleshly way, using our own power and armour and influence. The other, ' Unto us a Child is born.' All our working will be tried by fire. He prayed so beautifully with us, and his visit so refreshed us. He left in pelting rain for Kucheng.

" *Monday, May 27th.*—Hessie started . . for Kucheng.

" It was so hot that day, and, in time for dinner, Maud and Fanny arrived from Sangiong, meaning to stay with us till Wednesday, and then to leave for Kucheng, Foochow and Kuliang.[1] They had kept writing, asking me if I were not coming to Kuliang this summer, and saying, if so, I had better come with them and not wait to travel a month later by myself. I could not make up my mind what to do—whether to go to Hwasang with Flora and the others from Kucheng, or to come down to Kuliang and have a perfect change. The more Hessie and Lucy prayed about it, the more they felt I should come to Kuliang.

" However, that afternoon, as I was sitting in my study, feeling very dull, I heard Maud's step. You know the rest: that she told me I *was* to come with them down to Kuliang, and that I had better begin to pack at once.

[1] Kuliang is the summer resort on the hills above Foochow, as Hwasang is above Kucheng.

" All the next day I packed, dear little Lucy helping me so.[1]

" That evening Fanny's teacher spoke so beautifully on 'Looking unto Jesus.' One time the disciples were looking at the grandeur of the temple buildings. Another time their eyes were heavy with sleep and they could not look up to watch and pray.

" The devil tempts us to look at anything *but* Jesus. There was Stephen, who *was* looking up, and the devil was so angry, he did his best to get Stephen to look down, making the people wild until they stoned him. But nothing could make Stephen get his eyes down.

" Then when Jesus went up into heaven, the disciples' eyes were up. They were not looking at grand buildings then, they were not heavy with sleep, they were looking steadfastly up. So we must be looking ever unto Jesus.

" On *Wednesday, May* 29, we started. . . . Maud took all the responsibility. Fanny and I just looked on, and were taken in and done for. . . . Flora and Lucy were there, and the servants to help in the start, so it did all seem exciting.

" Finally I got in my chair and started, and Fanny came next, and Maud last, for she would always have us on in front.

" We got into Kucheng at 7.30 p.m., and found, of

---

[1] Little did any one think what the decision might have meant, if she had gone to Hwasang to be with Mr. and Mrs. Stewart, as Hessie Newcombe did, and shared their martyrdom.

course, only Hessie there to welcome us (to the ladies' house this means), the other sisters, you remember, being down in Foochow.

" Mrs. Stewart came in to see us that evening.

" *Thursday,* - *May* 30. We rested, and the dear little Stewarts all came in to see us, and I gave Herbert a dog and Evan a horse. You know those cardboard animals that —— sent me one time.

" In the afternoon we all went up to the Stewarts' for a prayer meeting. The American missionaries always come over for it if they are in Kucheng.

" We were all invited to the Stewarts' for supper. It was most nice, and Mrs. Stewart was sweet to me, calling me Annie.

" *Friday, May* 31. I took a quiet time. Nellie Saunders came in to see me. In the afternoon . . . Mrs. Stewart came in to tea. Chinese visitors came too, and I helped to talk to them.

" We had a walk on the hill, and in the evening Fanny's teacher preached again.

" *Saturday, June* 1. Talked over my second examination with Nellie Saunders, and then I went up to see Topsy, who was ill.

" *Sunday, June* 2. Fanny and I went to Sunday school and taught some women.

" Fanny's teacher preached on the Holy Spirit. It was Whit-Sunday. It was just a wonderful sermon. He said, God gave to us the Holy Spirit without limit, that it was *we* who said, Stop, I have enough.

" After dinner we went up to the Stewarts' (Mr. S.

F

was away itinerating). We sat in the garden and sang hymns.

"In the evening Fanny's teacher preached again. '*Take, take* the Holy Spirit; receive as much as ye will.'

"Hessie had said to me early in the morning, 'What a lovely day Whit-Sunday is; it is just *receiving*, opening our mouths wide and taking!

"*Monday, June* 3. Up at 5 a.m. . . . preparing for the long chair ride to the boat; but though the coolies arrived, they all refused to carry our baskets, saying they were too heavy, and, as it was hopeless, we had to send away the chair coolies too, for we could not start without our loads.

"After dinner Hessie started on a three weeks' itinerating tour.

"We went up and said good-bye to the Stewarts, and saw Mr. Stewart, who had just come back from his itinerating, so tired and hot. It was so sweet to see Mrs. Stewart's face, as she saw him coming in at the door so unexpectedly, and the little ones' joy and his joy in his children. . . .

"Maud, Fanny, and I returned to our house . . . To our joy the coolies returned, saying they would start with us. It being 4.30, we were making up our minds not to start till the next day. And the Stewarts had asked us in there to supper.

"However, we quickly locked up the house and started, leaving it quite empty, and sending the key to the Stewarts."

One or two more extracts I must give, omitting the journey (interesting and amusing as it is) to Foochow, where they stayed a few days, and the further travelling to Kuliang.

"*Kuliang, Thursday, June* 13. Splendid time in evening over Chinese prayers. We read round, and then all spoke on any verses that struck us . . Our servants and teachers are all Christians this year, so we do have such nice times over the Bible every evening—not just one person preaching, but all speaking and praying, as we like. . . .

"Flo Lloyd and Mabel Witherby arrived from Hing-hwa, very bright and sweet, but needing rest from all the heat they had come through."

Miss Alice Hankin writes from Dangseng Hing-hwa (the district south of Foochow) :—

"*May* 18, 1895. I must not forget to tell you we had such a delightful little visit from Mr. Stewart a fortnight ago. He was with us from Friday to Monday, and it was a real blessing to us and to our people.

"He preached on Sunday on *Love*, and it is nice to see how well the people have remembered his sermon."

"He being dead yet speaketh."

I cannot close this chapter better than by copying some verses from " Daily Light," which were brought to the minds of both Robert and Louisa Stewart in a remarkable way.

September 7, 1876, the day of their marriage, the texts were :—

" We must through much tribulation enter into the
kingdom of God." " Whosoever doth not bear his
cross and come after Me cannot be My disciple."

"No man should be moved by these afflictions: for
yourselves know that ye are appointed thereunto."

The following evening, *September* 8 :—

"Except a corn of wheat fall into the ground and
die, it abideth alone; but if it die, it bringeth forth
much fruit."

Again, on *September* 16, 1876, the day they left
London on the first journey to China :—

"No man should be moved by these afflictions, for
yourselves know that we are appointed thereunto, for
verily, when we were with you before we told you that
we should suffer persecution."

December 27, 1885, they left us again for China,
and the texts again spoke of suffering and glory :—

"Our light affliction . . . the exceeding weight
of glory."

" The sufferings of this present time are not worthy
to be compared to the glory that shall be revealed in
us."

September 1, 1893, they left us to go to China for
the last time. They had meetings in Canada on the
way. The same thoughts occur in the texts—suffering, glory. Robert often dwelt on the words, " To
you it is *given* . . . to suffer."

" If any man will come after Me, let him deny himself, and take up his cross and follow Me."

"Unto you it is *given* in the behalf of Christ not
only to believe, but also to suffer for His sake."

" If we suffer, we shall also reign with Him."

We had read these texts together, and applied them to the " trials of the way "—separation from children, etc. Now they seem prophetic.

We turned to "Daily Light " to see what verses they had last read ("Daily Light " was a *daily* companion), and we found the same message and encouragement.

July 31 :—

"Endure hardness as a good soldier of Jesus Christ."

"It became Him for whom are all things, and by whom are all things, in bringing many sons unto glory, to make the Captain of their salvation perfect through sufferings."

" We must through much tribulation enter the kingdom of God."

" The God of all grace, who hath called us unto His eternal glory by Christ Jesus, after that ye have suffered awhile, make you perfect, stablish, strengthen, settle you."

And on *August* 1 in the evening, after the telegram, we turned again to "Daily Light," and the Lord spoke to us—of them, still in the same tender keeping. The prophecy fulfilled, the suffering, thank God, over. The eternal glory begun, and to us, of " His pitiful, tender mercy "—

" The Lord is very pitiful, and of tender mercy."

" He that keepeth thee will not slumber."

" Behold He that keepeth Israel shall neither slumber nor sleep."

"His compassions fail not; they are new every morning."

"Truly His doctrine drops as the rain, His speech distils as the dew, as the small rain upon the tender herb, and as the showers upon the grass."

"His compassions fail not."

"God is Love."

CHAPTER IV

THE JOYFUL SOUND

"How shall they hear without a preacher?"—ROM. x. 14.

CHAPTER IV

THE JOYFUL SOUND

I COR. i. 23, 24.

O, that Thy Name may be sounded
　Afar over earth and sea,
Till the dead awaken and praise Thee
　And the dumb lips sing to Thee !
Sound forth as a song of triumph
　Wherever man's foot has trod,
The despised, the derided message,
　The foolishness of God.
Jesus, dishonoured and dying,
　A felon on either side—
Jesus, the song of the drunkards,
　Jesus the crucified !
　　Name of God's tender comfort,
　　Name of His glorious power,
　　Name that is song and sweetness,
　　The strong everlasting tower.
　　Jesus the Lamb accepted,
　　Jesus the Priest on His throne—
　　Jesus the King who is coming —
　　Jesus, Thy Name alone !

C. P. C.[1]

I HAVE tried to divide the work of the native Bible-women and the English ladies of the C.E.Z.M.S. "Foreign women," enquirers call them

---

[1] In " Hymns of Tersteegen, Suso and others," by Mrs. Bevan.

—" dear ku-niongs" is the Christian name for them; but among the heathen they are known and feared as " foreign devils."

But God has so joined together these two agencies, that in telling the story of His work among the women of China they cannot be " put asunder."

In the foregoing chapter about the native Bible-women, much has been told in Mrs. Stewart's own words, of the need—and how that need has been partially supplied—of English sisters who will come and work shoulder to shoulder with their less-favoured sisters in China.

But, oh, how she longed for reinforcements! Mrs. Ahok used to wonder why all the " ku-niongs" (un-married women) could not go to China. I have heard her question a young lady:

" You love Jesus?"

" Yes."

" You go China? "—with an eager, longing look, followed by one of disappointed hope, when a shake of the head gave a decided refusal. Alas! Mrs. Ahok did not understand that all the " ku-niongs" in England who think they love Jesus have not sought and obtained the promised power to make them witnesses, first " in Jerusalem," and then in ever-widening circles, " to the uttermost parts of the earth " (Acts i. 8).

Mr. and Mrs. Stewart prayed often and earnestly, not only for missionaries, but that those only who were really called, and specially prepared by God, might go.

Not quantity, but quality. "Not by might" (margin, army) "nor by power, but by My Spirit, saith the Lord of Hosts."

MRS. AHOK'S STORY. BY MRS. STEWART.

1890. When first Miss Foster began to visit the family of Mr. Ahok, a rich Chinese merchant at Foochow, there seemed little hope that the good seed would ever find an entrance into their hearts. Mrs. Ahok herself, her mother, mother-in-law, two daughters-in-law, and step-daughters, were all worshipping idols, and quite satisfied with them, and, as they say now, without any desire for God. Mr. Ahok alone was seeking for light, and was anxious that his family should have some teaching. English was the only thing his wife had any wish to learn, and she consented, for the sake of this, to read the Bible with Miss Foster, and to permit her to have a Bible-class at her house once a week for the other members of the family.

Long and patiently Miss Foster laboured, sowing the seed, but with apparently little result, till at last illness visited the family; one little child died—a grandson of Mr. Ahok's—and little Charlie, Mr. Ahok's adopted son, was so ill that the Chinese doctor said there was no hope of saving his life. Miss Foster went to the house and offered to stay and nurse the child herself. They were unwilling at first, but at last consented, thinking it would not make much difference what the foreign lady did, as the child must

die in any case.   However, it pleased God to spare the
life of the little one, to the great joy of the family, and
from that time a decided change took place: much of
their former bitterness and opposition passed away,
and Miss Foster was looked upon as a real friend.

Still some time elapsed before any signs appeared
that the seed had fallen into good ground.   In answer
to prayer, a little son was given to Mrs. Ahok, as told
in the little book called a " Remarkable Answer to
Prayer," and from his birth he was given to God and
called the "Christian child."   Not long afterwards
Mr. Ahok was himself baptized, then his wife and
daughter, and one daughter-in-law; and later on Mrs.
Ahok's own mother, who, of all the family, had been
the most bitterly opposed to Christianity, became a
true and earnest believer in the Lord Jesus, and
showed even in her face the great change that had
taken place within.

I wish I could give you, in Mrs. Ahok's own words,
her account of this great change in her life, as she
told it to a small gathering of Chinese women to cheer
and encourage them.   What I remember of it is as
follows :—

"I never thought of God, nor had any desire after
Him, but in His great love and mercy He had compassion on me, and sent one of His servants to me to
my own home.   It was Miss Foster.

" At first I could not understand her message, and
my heart was all in darkness, but by-and-by the light
began to shine: it was, as you have often seen at

sunrise, first a faint light when nothing is seen distinctly, then the sun itself appears, and in a flood of light all is clear.

"So it was in my heart when Christ came in. All my doubts and fears vanished, and I found a joy and peace I never knew before. But my difficulty then was to confess that I was a follower of the Lord Jesus, a member of the despised band of Christians. I felt I would rather die than acknowledge it, and was tempted to think I might worship Christ in secret.

"But this also I took to the Saviour, and told Him my weakness and fear of confessing I was His servant; and "—she concluded, her face beaming with joy—"He took it all away, and I now feel neither fear nor shame, and it is my greatest joy to go to the houses of my rich friends, and plead with them to give up their idols, and find the same peace that I have found in serving Christ."

Mr. Ahok was the first to manifest his anxiety about their rich friends in the city of Foochow, and he invited Miss F. to go with him to visit the ladies. She did so, and was kindly received in many houses, and begged to come again and tell them about the Saviour of whom they had never before heard. But she was not able to make much use of the opportunities thus offered her, for she was soon obliged to leave China on account of ill-health. She had seen enough, however, to convince her that the ground was ready for the seed, if only there were sowers ready to go forth.

The C.E.Z.M.S. were then entreated to extend
their pity to the women of China as they had done to
" India's Women," and their answer was to send out a
lady (Miss Gough), who quickly learned the language,
and began to visit the ladies in the city with great
energy. Mrs. Ahok accompanied her in these visits,
and introduced her to many families of high rank and
position. Owing to Miss Gough's teaching and influence, Mrs. Ahok herself also rapidly advanced in
knowledge, and became as earnest as her husband
in seeking to bring the knowledge of the Gospel to
her friends and neighbours.

Miss Gough, however, was not permitted to see
much result of her " seed-sowing " in Foochow. She
was called away before long to another field of labour,
and now, as Mrs. Hoare, she is working as earnestly
for the women at Ningpo as she formerly did at
Foochow.

The C.E.Z.M.S., however, did not give up China,
and soon sent out two ladies (the Misses Newcombe)
to fill Miss Gough's place ; and, about a year later,
they were followed by two more (Miss Bradshaw and
Miss Davies).

The Misses Newcombe's special work is in the
country, in the Kucheng district, about 120 miles
from Foochow, where they have more on their hands
than they can possibly accomplish, and Miss Bradshaw and Miss Davies have been obliged, up to the
present, to give most of their time to the study of the
language ; still they have done what they could to

keep up the visiting among the ladies in the city, accompanied by Mrs. Ahok. Miss Davies hopes to take up these Chinese ladies as her special work, and Miss Bradshaw writes encouragingly of the openings they are having. She says: "When in the city on Saturday we had many *invitations* to large houses, which we had been definitely praying for, as Mr Ahok said we must wait to be asked before going to large houses. One very rich family had heard of us, and asked to be allowed to come to our house to see us. On Monday we were invaded by seven very grand city ladies, escorted by gentlemen on horseback. They stayed all day; they had *never* heard 'The Old, Old Story,' and never seen foreigners. Mrs. Ahok was greatly cheered at such a perfectly new door being opened; she and Chitnio talked turn about, and we had plenty of singing."

Mrs. Ahok also writes to the same effect:—" My mother-in-law died last year in August, as you have heard, and while I was in mourning Chinese custom would not allow me to go among the higher class of people in the city; they would not like it, and it would hurt their feelings; but I have been once into the city with Miss Davies to see the ladies you used to call upon with me. Their tribe is Ling; they were enquiring about you; I hope soon to go among these people again in the city. I often go to the houses near my house. Yesterday Mrs. Ling (Chitnio) and I went to visit some people; they were very nice, and quite interested in what we told them about this doctrine.

Several of them asked us to come again, so we are going this afternoon. Once a week I have Prayer Meetings at the Hospital with the sick women there. We pray God to bless the words that have been spoken, that they may bring forth fruit to His glory. My mother is quite happy since she became a Christian; she lives next door to me, and it is easy for her to come to me when she likes. My nephew's family also know the doctrine very well, only they have not come out, but some of them come to the Prayer Meetings very often. I hope that before long they may come out and confess Christ before all men."

As we trace the story of Mrs. Ahok from the beginning, ought we not to praise God, and take courage for the future? Paul may plant and Apollos water, but it is God alone who gives the increase, and in answer to prayer He can and will bless these ladies in Foochow city, and make them chosen instruments to spread the knowledge of His Truth.

Mrs. Ling writes: "I know you are all praying for China, but please pray specially for Foochow city; though the walls are great and the people strong, we have a King who is stronger than they; He can break down those great walls; we must only have *great faith* in God. He can do it. There is nothing too hard for Him. "Not by might nor by power, but by My Spirit, saith the Lord of Hosts."

So far we have been only thinking of the work among the *rich* Chinese, but God is also working among the poorer classes; indeed in China, as elsewhere, we see how true are the words of the Apostle, uttered long ago, "Hath not God chosen the poor of this world, *rich* in faith." The seed sown, though apparently in hopelessly dull and hard hearts, He has caused to spring up and bear fruit. The School for Women at Foochow and the Boarding School for Girls have been the means of sowing the seed. At Kucheng, too, there is now a school for both women and girls. During Mrs. Banister's absence in England the elder Miss Newcombe takes charge of the women, and the younger the girls. They also visit ·the Bible-women at the country stations, occasionally spending a few days or a week in one of the villages, where they have splendid opportunities of giving instruction to the Christians, and of talking to the heathen women who come in crowds to see the foreign ladies.

Let me give you some instances of the results of this " seed-sowing." From our Foochow School already sixty women have gone back to their heathen villages, carrying with them the knowledge of the truth : sixteen of these are Bible-women, giving up their whole time to work among their heathen sisters, others are wives of the Catechists at the mission stations, and others, again, are wives of the ordinary Christian men in the country congregations, who are glad to come for a time to learn a little of God's Word, and many of these have been the means of great blessing on their return to their own villages. I should like to tell you of one of these dear women

G

who has now passed away to be with the Master she so faithfully served.

Many years ago a woman came to us from a distant country village. She had heard of the doctrine, but knew nothing very clearly about it. She longed to learn more, so she begged her friends to allow her to go to Foochow to be taught. They tried to shake her resolution by frightening her in every way they could, but, finding her determined, at last consented to let her go. A short time after her arrival some men and boys came from her village to pay her a visit to see if anything dreadful had happened to her, but, finding her well and happy, they returned home a good deal re-assured.

The dear old woman spent some time in our school, learning most diligently the difficult Chinese characters, and when she had finished her time, she went out as a Bible-woman. She worked at first in the Ning-taik district, and afterwards became matron of the Women's School at Fuh-ning, superintended by Mrs. Martin, and she was there remarkable for her earnestness about the souls of all the women with whom she came in contact. Some little time ago she was taken ill, and after a time of great bodily suffering, went in to "see the King." Mrs. Martin writes of her: "Perhaps you have heard of our great loss in the death of Mrs. Ling Ming Ching. I may say I *daily* miss her; it is just six weeks since we laid her to rest in our hill Cemetery looking over the sea . . . She suffered excessively, but always said,

Sing-ta cheng k'i-k'wi, sing-tie ping-ang,' ' the body is very miserable ; the heart is peace.' "

One other case I might mention. A young woman came to the school by the wish of her husband, who was then a student in the college. She was a heathen, and was very angry with him for becoming a Christian, and was bitterly opposed to Christianity. Mrs. Ling writes of her in a letter recently received : " The Siu-gie huoi-sing is wonderfully earnest. Do you remember when she came to the Women's School she was unconverted, and not willing to learn ; wanted to go home very much; and then her little boy got very ill, and Miss Gough sent for Dr. Corey to see him ? She was very sad for her child, and we prayed with her in her room that God would spare his life, and that his mother might give her heart to Christ, and train him up for God. He did answer those prayers; the child is quite well, and the mother is much nicer, cheered, and brighter, growing in grace every day. She asked for baptism, and was baptized, and now she is very earnest, and likes to go out whenever the Bible-woman goes.

" She has two children ; sometimes she leaves them at home, and sometimes she takes one with her. In the evening she helps her husband in the subjects for examination at the Conference."

Our Annual Meetings for the Native Female Workers, who come from the country stations, where they are working often amid difficulties and discouragement, are times of refreshment and blessing to all.

Of one of these meetings, Mrs. Lloyd, now in charge of the Foochow Women's School, writes: " Our Conference is just over, and you will be glad to know that we had some happy meetings with the women. . . . Fourteen women came from the country, besides Lydia, and one or two more from the city. Mrs. Chung Seng came; we thought it would be well for her to do so, as she has the Women's School at Hinghwa. It was very cheering to see so many of the old faces again, and I think they all enjoyed being together."

Mrs. Ling also sends an account of some of the meetings. She says: " We enjoyed the meetings very much, and I think they have done us all good, and quite refreshed us for work again. All the Bible-women up in the country have done their best; they all gave accounts of their work this year. In some places they have had very nice opportunities; some women have been brought to Christ, but in others the heathen said many bad things to them. Do you remember Ong-ai? She is the best of all. She has visited many places, and has had a very good time, and several women have become Christians, and are willing to unbind their feet. I am very thankful to see her so earnest. She used to go with Miss Newcombe, Mrs. Seng-mi, and two Christian women, to visit."

Thank God the "good seed" is being sown, and God is blessing the sowers, and is sending forth more of His children to join in this great work. Two new

workers were added to the number last autumn—
Miss Apperson, who has had two years' experience
of work in Ireland in connection with the Irish Church
Missions, and Miss Johnson, whose three years' training as a nurse will make her help specially valuable
in opening up new work. She was, therefore, chosen
to work in the Kiong-ning district, in the north-west
of the Fuhkien province, a large tract of country
containing several million inhabitants, but where as
yet the C.M.S. have only two missionaries.

One other lady, Miss Nesbit, has joined the band
of workers, sent to China by friends in Australia, in
connection with the C.E.Z.M.S., making the number
seven, or rather did make seven, for since I began
to write this paper a telegram has come from China,
saying Miss Bradshaw is even now on her way home,
as she had been suffering in her health for some time.
Six ladies! And what is the extent of the work
before them? Foochow city, with its half-million
inhabitants, would seem in itself more than enough.
We should not think six lady workers too many for
one of our great cities at home, with all the other
countless agencies at work in them; but besides the
city there are villages innumerable within easy reach,
and beyond, on the north and south, three large
districts, Lieng-kong, Lo-nguong, and Hok-chiang,
where the women are longing for teachers. Then
toward the north-west the immense district of Kucheng, with its large city, and numerous towns and
villages; Ping-nang district, almost equal to it in size;

and beyond these again the great Kiong-ning Prefecture, with its *seven* counties, almost all still in utter
heathen darkness.

Can only *six* be spared from home to bring the
Gospel to these millions of Chinese women? Must
hundreds of thousands pass into eternity, and never
hear of our Saviour's great love in dying for them,
because the followers of Christ are not willing to take
up the Cross and follow in His footsteps? The path
He trod led down step by step from the Father's throne
to the place of a servant, and at last to "death, even
the death of the Cross," and thus He brought salvation
to the world, and we cannot faithfully follow Him
without sacrifice of some kind.

May some at least who read this paper willingly
offer themselves to follow in the footsteps of our
Blessed Master, and give themselves, their lives, if
need be, for the salvation of the heathen. The Lord
is still pleading, "Whom shall I send, and who will
go for us?" Will you not joyfully accept the invitation, saying, "Here am I; send me"? looking forward
with hope to the fulfilment of the glorious promise,
"He that goeth forth and weepeth, bearing precious
seed, shall doubtless come again with rejoicing, bringing his sheaves with him."

Some extracts from letters written by Mrs. Stewart
in 1894 and early in 1895, show very clearly what
she felt about the dear missionary sisters already in
the field, and her earnest desire that others might join
them.

" KUCHENG, *February* 16, 1894.

" Benjamina Newcombe and L. Bryer left us yesterday; Miss Codrington and Miss Tolley started this morning for Sa-iong. I wonder if I told you about A. Tolley going there.

" Sa-iong is a town about a day's journey from here. About a year ago it was opened as a Z.M.S. station. Miss Codrington, F. Burroughs, and Maude Newcombe, went to live there.

" The people were most friendly, and the openings for work excellent.

" Miss Codrington is just beginning a girls' day school, and a class for women.

" Maude Newcombe, however, moved on to a large town called Sang-iong, half a day's journey. She found such readiness to hear, that she has spent some months there alone.

" Now she wants F. Burroughs to go and live there with her; R. has consented to their working there for one year, and then they must move on to a more destitute place! We have so few ladies we cannot afford to let them live within half a day's journey of each other!

" Miss Weller has the girls' school . . . and visiting in the villages around.

" A. Nesbit has the babies—eighteen of them—and one section of the district to visit, which means about twelve stations where there are catechists, and each of these centres for other towns and villages simply endless.

"Lucy Stewart has another section about equal in size, Elsie Marshall another.

"Leaving only Annie Gordon for the whole of Ping-nang! Besides all this there are women to be taught here, and R. much wants help in teaching in the boys' school. Twenty-five boarders we expect next term, and each boy is to pay $6 a year. So we are coming on in self-support, are we not?

"The girls too are making a beginning: they are to give $1 a term. So people cannot say they become Christians for what they get!"

In another letter dated April 30, 1894, also from Kucheng, she tells again to another friend about Sa-iong, telling how Miss Codrington has been living there for a year.

"The opportunities for work there are also *most* encouraging.

"She has a day school for children, and is welcomed in almost every house in the place. In five villages round good work is springing up, and she has lately had a very good 'Station Class.' . . . She gathers women anxious to be taught and keeps them three months, giving them their food only. She began with six women, and she says all these six have expressed their desire to follow Jesus, and have witnessed bravely in their homes. Two have already unbound their feet and two more are preparing to do so.

"Annie Gordon (a really first-rate little missionary — we like her greatly) has just come back from spending a month in the Ping-nang district.

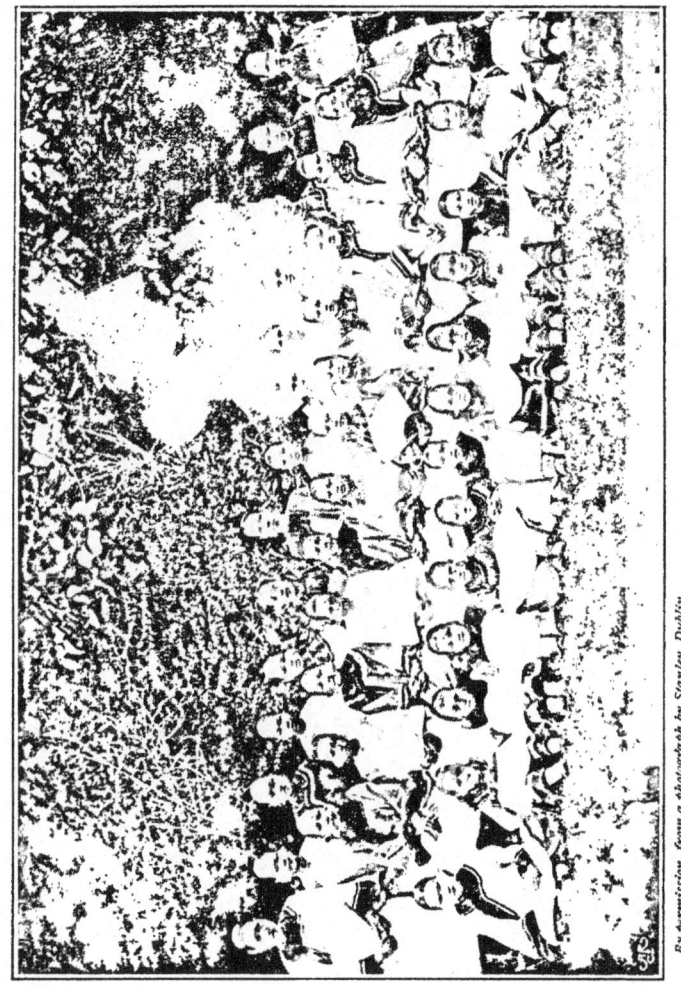

By permission, from a photograph by Stanley, Dublin.

Boarding School at Kucheng, begun by Miss Hessie Newcombe.

" At Dong-gio a most interesting work is going on.

" About fifty women come regularly to the services. We have had a Bible-woman there who has taught them a good deal, but you can fancy what such women must need—' line upon line, precept upon precept.'

" Annie Gordon had a most happy time there. Nine women came daily to be taught, and she had more invitations than she could accept to go to their houses to see them. Dong-gio is about a day's journey from here northward. A day further on, still going north, is another town called Dong-kau. Robert spent a Sunday there, and found the people so open for the message that he asked Miss Gordon to go on there for a few days, which she did, accompanied by a Bible-woman, and they had a splendid time. We are going to send the Bible-woman there for a month, and then Miss Gordon will go again and make a longer stay.

" We have twenty-four boys in the school, who pay $6 a year. I take the head class every morning for an hour and a half. Such nice lads they are. I *do* enjoy teaching them.

" We have no women's school this term.[1]

" A number of women come to Sunday-school and church, and from the villages all round invitations come—more than can be attended to. In the city (Ku-cheng) the openings seem endless."

From another letter, dated Hwasang, August 11, 1894, we give an extract :—

[1] A house was built soon after. The money having been sent by friends, through her mother, Mrs. Smyly.

"We are so looking forward to dear Hessie New-combe coming back in the autumn. Every one loves her, and she is a good influence wherever she goes. *Do* pray that the Lord may send more workers. . . . We simply don't know how to plan the work for next winter with our small numbers."

In a letter dated Kucheng, January 2, 1895, she again pleads for more workers to a friend greatly interested. Mentioning again about the ladies and their districts, she says :—

"We have two at Sang-iong, quite out of reach; two more a long day's journey from us.

"Then we have four who make Kucheng their headquarters, but they are seldom here more than a few days at a time—at least, three of them; the fourth, Miss Weller, has the boarding school, with fifty-four girls, and the babies too, now Miss Nesbit has gone on furlough. Each of these girls has an area of about 300 square miles! Annie Gordon, indeed, far more; she is the only lady-worker in Ping-nang.

"Next term we hope to have the women's school open, with about twenty women to be taught, and I have the boys' school to a great extent on my hands, as Robert is so constantly away. So you see we have plenty of room for more workers, and we are con-tinually laying the matter before the Lord."

The home for babies mentioned in the letters was begun by Miss Hessie Newcombe, and supported mainly, I believe, by her friends.

The inmates are the little girl-babies doomed to

death by their parents, who think they are of no value. But He who said, " suffer the *little* children to come," put it into the hearts of some of the " ku-niongs " to receive the rejected mites, and bring them up to love the Saviour who was despised and rejected for our sakes.

Mr. Simpson, that sweet singer of New York, when travelling in China, saw the body of a little baby-girl floating face downwards in a canal. I venture to quote some of his stanzas.

May God write the touching appeal on all our hearts.

> " Only a little baby girl
>   Dead by the river side ;
> Only a little Chinese child
>   Drowned in the floating tide.
>
> If she had only been a boy,
>   They would have heard her cry ;
> But she was just a baby-girl,
>   And she was left to die.
>
> So they have left her little form
>   Floating upon the wave :
> She was too young to have a soul,
>   Why should she have a grave ?
>
> Yes, and there's many another lamb
>   Perishing every day,
> Thrown by the road or the river side,
>   Flung to the beasts of prey.
>
> Is there a mother's heart to-night
>   Clasping her darling child,
> Willing to leave these helpless lambs
>   Out on the desert wild ?

Is there a little Christian girl,
    Happy in love and home,
Living in selfish ease, while they
    Out on the mountains roam?

Think as you lie on your little cot,
    Smoothed by a mother's hand ;
Think of the little baby-girls
    Over in China's land.

Ask if there is not something more
    Even a child can do,
And if perhaps in China's land
    Jesus has need of you.

Only a little baby-girl
    Dead by the river side ;
Only a little Chinese child
    Drowned in the floating tide.

But it has brought a vision vast,
    Dark as a nation's woe ;
Oh ! has it left some willing heart
    Answering ' I will go ' ? "

Letter from China by Rev. R. W. Stewart.

"Kucheng, Foochow, China,
      "*November* 20, 1894.

" I have been wishing to tell you something of the work of your ladies in the Fuhkien province, which I have myself seen in the past year.

" My wife and I reached Foochow from Canada just a year ago, and before coming up to our inland station we spent a week at the Treaty Port of Foochow.

" Here we found five of your ladies hard at work, three of them living at the Z.M.S. ' Olives ' — Miss

Mead, Miss Strong, and Miss Stevens. To the first-
named is committed the work among women in the
city of Foochow. There are in the city about half
a million people, and she is the only one of your ladies
that can be spared. She has rented a small house in
one of the main thoroughfares; in the lower part of
it she has a Girls' Day School, and in the upper part
she spends four days out of each week, returning to
the 'Olives' for the other three days. In the city
she finds a great number of houses open to her, more
than she is able to visit. The women receive her
very gladly, but their husbands too often, on finding
their wives being really influenced, take fright, and
forbid further visits. There are great possibilities in
this work, but it has peculiar difficulties, and calls
for your prayers.

" Miss Strong's sphere of work has been the Women's
Training School in Foochow. She has had generally
as many as twenty women, almost all from the Hok-
chiang district, the other more distant districts having
their own institutions.

" No work is more important than this of training
women—fitting them to be themselves teachers—and
Miss Strong has devoted herself to it with the greatest
energy, and, I may say, courage; for, owing to her
failing eyesight, she has often been tempted to give
it up, but has yet bravely held on till, alas! the doctor
would allow her to stay no longer in the country, and
she has returned home, every one in the Mission
hoping it may be but for a time.

"The third inmate of the 'Olives,' Miss Stevens, sent out by the Tasmanian Y.W.C.A.—Mrs. Fagg, formerly one of our missionaries here, being one of the leading spirits in that association; unable to return to the work she loved so much, she has sent out already two substitutes, and we are grateful. Miss Stevens divides her time between village work on the Nantai Island, and attending to the needs of the up-country sisters, who now number more than twenty, and who get all their home correspondence, stores, etc., etc., through her. What time she has left from these she gives to visiting in the large Foochow hospital.

"In Foochow you have also a Girls' Boarding School, rapidly increasing in number, under the charge of Miss Leslie, with whom Miss Lee is living while learning the language. This little school is intended to reach the upper-class children whom Miss Mead is able to influence in the city, and some do belong to this class, though not all. The rule is for them to pay the greater portion of the expense of their food and clothes, but Miss Leslie is sometimes obliged to relax a little. From about twenty children last year, it has increased to nearly double that number now, and who can tell what good may come from the messages these children will bring back to their homes, dark heathen homes, in that most sinful city, Foochow?

"You have two more workers in Foochow who must not be forgotten, Miss Barr and Miss Chambers.

They are stationed in the native hospital, which is under the care of Dr. Rennie. Although it is not a Mission Hospital, Dr. Rennie gives the ladies full scope for influencing the patients. Were it·actually a Mission Hospital, they could not have more freedom in speaking to and teaching the inmates. Although they only reached Foochow last March, they are able to make their ideas known in Chinese very fairly, and when I saw them the other day they told me how happy they were, and what a splendid sphere of work they found theirs to be. On their arrival, at Dr. Rennie's suggestion, a Sunday service was commenced, and now so many come it is often hard to find room for them. On Tuesday, too, there is a service, now conducted by Mr. Bannister ; and our old friend, Mrs. Ahok, holds a weekly meeting for the women patients in the room where her good husband used to get the men together. I ought to have said that I found Mrs. Ahok giving much assistance to Miss Leslie. Her house is close by the school, and every day she takes a class of the girls, and is also instrumental in bringing the greater number of them to the school.

"The next district, north of Foochow, where you have ladies working, is Lo-ngnong. Here your new house, at a village called Uong-buang, is just completed, and I think will be one of the most suitable in the Mission for the purpose. It is entirely native in its external appearance, while within it is slightly altered from the ordinary Chinese building. It will take in three ladies easily, and the entire cost, includ-

H

ing furniture, will not exceed £80. Miss Hook and
Miss Cooper are just about moving in, and it is intended that your new lady, Miss Wedderspoon, should
join them. Miss Hook has already been itinerating
frequently through the district, and speaks of it as
very happy work, and full of opportunities for usefulness. Up to the present there has practically been
no itinerating by ladies in that important district.
There are a good number of new converts, but the
women have had nothing done for them. Mrs. Martin,
whose death the whole Mission so deeply regret, had
a Women's School. This was an excellent institution,
but beyond this there was nothing, for there were no
ladies to take up the work till your Society came to
its aid two years ago.

"Travelling south from Foochow, between two and
three days' journey, you reach Hing-hwa. In this
district you have two stations, the one at Dang-seng,
and the other, a day and a half distant, at Sieng-iu.
This district is unique among all the districts of the
Mission, for it is practically self-supporting, there
only being at present one catechist paid from Mission
Funds, the other catechists being supported by the
Christians themselves, who have put up their own
places of worship, and who flock to them on Sundays
in large numbers. The opportunities for work among
the women at these two stations of yours is quite
wonderful. Miss Hankin has written telling you of
it. She, with Miss Witherby, at Dang-seng, have
given most of their time that they could spare from

learning the language to itinerations through the surrounding country, and holding weekly classes for instruction. Now they are about to start a Women's School, where Christian women will be trained, and then sent back to their own villages to work among their countrywomen, in the first place entirely unpaid: possibly later on one or two may be selected as specially fitted for the post of Bible-woman. The Society has excellent premises here, and recently Miss Hankin's friends have provided funds for the building of the Women's School.

" Your other station in the Hing-hwa district, Siengiu, is occupied by Miss Lloyd and Miss Tabberer, both from the town of Leicester, and here, too, a Women's School has been started in a small way. Next year it is to be enlarged, and the expense will be borne by a good friend in the cause in Leicester.

" Three days' journey west from Foochow is our station of Kucheng, to which is joined the district of Ping-nang, the two together covering an area equal to about half the size of Wales, and as populous as the rest of China. In this region you have now two fixed stations, Kucheng and Sa-iong, a long day's journey separating them and two other stations, which for the greater part of the year have ladies in them.

" Kucheng.—Here Miss Nisbet is in charge of the Foundling Institution, which takes in poor little girl-babies cast off by their parents. The numbers have increased, till we had to give notice no more could be taken in. Miss Nisbet gives nearly all her time to mothering these little things.   There are in all about thirty, some of them out at nurse.

" There is also a large district allotted to Miss Nisbet, covering some 200 square miles, with little bands of Christians dotted here and there through it, the women sorely needing looking up and teaching, but they can get very little.   Another institution here is the Girls' Boarding School, in charge of Miss Weller.   This, too, has so increased that, though the school was enlarged considerably last year, it is now again quite full, and this, too, in spite of a new rule by which they must each pay a fixed portion of the expenses, and also must all of them unbind their feet.   There are now close on sixty of these girls, and if they fulfil the hopes of their teachers, they will do much towards elevating and Christianizing the country.

" I ought to say that the Foundling Institution was built at the expense of an Irish clergyman, and is being supported entirely by individual friends.   And so this Girls' School was erected, and is supported in a similar manner, neither institution drawing anything from the Society's funds.

" The three other ladies who regard Kucheng as their headquarters are Miss Gordon, Miss Marshall, and Miss Stewart.   The last-named is still working for her examinations, and when she has got through them, her work will be in the country, in the western section of the district.   Miss Gordon's station, where she spends the greater part of the year, is Dong-gio, the Mission chief centre for the Ping-nang district.

This great district, or, as we would say in England, county, has no other lady worker but this one, and I need not say that though she works ever so hard, she can but barely touch what is waiting to be done. At that one station of Dong-gio there is a usual attendance of eighty or ninety women at the Sunday services. We have to thank Rev. H. B. Macartney for this valuable missionary. I only hope he will be able to send us some more like her.

"Miss Marshall's work is also in the country, only returning now and then to Kucheng as headquarters. Her section lies north of Kucheng, and covers more than 300 square miles. She has several centres in this region, where she stops for a few weeks or two months at a time, collecting the women together, and visiting from house to house. The plan is for the sisters to travel in twos, accompanied by a Bible-woman and a Christian servant, and to put up at chapels where there is stationed a married catechist. Just now she is at a place called Sek-ce-du (with Miss Saunders, of the Australian C.M.A., who is stationed with us while learning the language), and a letter has come in to-day from her, telling of the great encouragement they are having in that place, which hitherto has been utterly dead, although we have again and again endeavoured to arouse an interest. Thank God for these dear sisters! Wherever they go God gives His blessing.

"Their secret is quiet unwavering trust in the Saviour by their side, and He does not fail them.

"Your other fixed station in this Kucheng district is Sa-long, where Miss Codrington and Miss Tolley are located, the latter still learning the language, but at the same time doing many useful little bits of work. I took the Bishop here on his recent confirmation tour, and he seemed specially impressed by the good work he saw doing.

"The chief feature in Miss Codrington's work is her 'Station Class.' This is a new departure in our Mission, and she is the first to try it. The idea is to gather a class of women from neighbouring villages, and keep them for three months at a time with her in her house, teaching them day by day, assisted by a well-instructed Bible-woman, the great fundamental truths of Christianity, and the chief incidents of the Bible, and then sending them back to their homes, to be voluntary workers among their people.

"It was thought by many that three months' teaching would be of little use for these ignorant minds, but experience has shown quite the reverse. I examined one of her three months' classes, and was delighted at their answering, so utterly different from the ordinary untaught women. They had learned not only a number of facts, but they had learned to think, and it was a delightful surprise to find how thoroughly they understood the truth, and how intelligently they were able to answer.

"Then besides the 'Station Class,' Miss Codrington visits regularly the surrounding villages within a radius of six or eight miles, sometimes travelling even

further, and holding little classes in these places, and
thus Sa-long, from being so hopeless a station that we
had actually withdrawn our catechist from it, has
now a congregation of from fifty to a hundred, and
the interest is steadily increasing. There is a little
Girls' Day School here too, daily taught by Miss
Tolley, and they answered well at their examination.

"Ten miles still further east, across the mountains,
lies the town of Sang-long, and here Miss Maud Newcombe and Miss Burroughs have been working for a
year. Here, too, have 'Station Classes' been held, a
Girls' School established, and villages visited, just as
I have described at Sa-long, and visible and wonderful success has in the same way followed. The work
is really done in their little room upstairs, where the
two sisters kneel together so many times a day.

"Miss Newcombe's furlough is due, and she has not
been very strong, and many think she should take a
rest; but the Christians hearing of it, have drawn up
petitions, one of which they laid before the Bishop,
begging that she might stay on among them yet
another year, and I rather think she is going to yield.
I trust it may not be at the expense of her health.
So far from European intercourse, one would suppose their lot must be a sad one, and yet, like the
other sisters, they firmly maintain that they never,
even in the dear home-lands, had before such happy
work. 'Go . . . and lo, I AM WITH YOU always,'
accounts for this otherwise inexplicable fact.

"There only remains to speak of the far North-West,

where Nang-ua is the Mission centre for your ladies. It is four days' journey over high mountains from Ku-cheng. I visited them at the beginning of the year, and found there Miss Johnson, Miss B. Newcombe, Miss Rodd, Miss Bryer, Miss Fleming; they have also among them a Miss Sinclair, who has come from England independently, and is making herself useful in various ways. These devoted ladies are living as nearly like the native women as possible; no knives or forks are seen in the house. I am told there is one knife kept for any unhappy guest who cannot manage with chop sticks, and though the locality is far from a healthy one, and our C.M.S. missionaries have one after another felt the effects of the malaria, your ladies have wonderfully maintained their strength. You know the kind of life they lead, visiting from village to village, sometimes at long distances from home, putting up, not at chapels or Christians' houses, for alas! there are none, but in the native inn, or the house of some hospitable heathen woman; and God is using them. It is truly invigorating to the soul to sit down and listen to these devoted ladies telling of the spiritual work they have themselves witnessed.

"Oh, for more of these 'women that publish the tidings.' They have, too, a little hospital here in Miss Johnson's charge, and they have also been able to start a small 'Station Class,' though in doing so they had to face difficulties which were not met with in the older districts.

"And now, in drawing this long letter to a conclusion, I must say that with all these ladies are doing before one's eyes, and the utter devotion of their lives, it *was* a disappointment to observe in the Annual Report that your 'China Fund' was at so low an ebb, the receipts last year being less than the expenditure by £900, so that the balance in hand is almost gone. What is Fuhkien to do this coming year? Unless funds come in quite unexpectedly, there will be a great deficit.

" Do your readers know that China only gets money sent in specially marked as for China ? If they did, I don't believe they could leave the 'China Fund' to languish like this. These dear sisters, who, as you know, are all of them on the reduced rate of salary, wrote to me on observing this in your Report, that they felt they must themselves try to help still further. One said, 'I will pay our Mission messenger myself.' Another said, 'I will pay my teacher.' Two others, 'We will pay the rent of our Mission House,' etc. They will not lose by it. 'There is that scattereth and yet increaseth.' 'The Lord *loveth* a cheerful giver.'

" One good result is this, your 'China Fund' is now being remembered in prayer as never before, and He who has the silver and the gold will certainly give what is needed.

" ROBERT W. STEWART."

Mr. Stewart's letter to the Committee of the C.E.Z.M.S. will be read with interest. He describes the "foreign women" no longer "strangers and foreigners," but at home in the hearts of the Chinese women.

And are not his closing words as "a voice out of the cloud" to us now, pleading that lack of funds should not be a reason why missionaries must not be sent to China?

Is it true that—as a living writer has said—we Christians have been "electro-plated with avarice"—taking care of ourselves, providing for our own families, taking thought what we shall eat and what we shall drink, and wherewithal we shall be clothed, and turning a deaf ear to the bitter cry of millions who are starving for the Bread of Life?

Jesus Christ died for them as much as for us.

He has already told us to go and preach this good news to *every creature.*

If we neglect to do this, will He not say to us,—

"Thou oughtest therefore to have put My money to the exchangers, and then at My coming I should have received Mine own with usury?"

Oh! may no one who reads this book have the solemn words that follow addressed to them,—"Take therefore the talent from him . . . and cast ye the unprofitable servant into outer darkness."

"Wherefore He saith, Awake, thou that sleepest, and arise from the dead, and Christ shall give thee light. . . . And be not drunk with wine, wherein is excess; but BE FILLED WITH THE SPIRIT."

CHAPTER V

NATIVE BOYS AND GIRLS AT SCHOOL

" Esaias is very bold, and saith, I was found of them that sought
Me not."—ROM. x. 20

CHAPTER V

NATIVE BOYS AND GIRLS AT SCHOOL

From the glory and the gladness,
  From His secret place;
From the rapture of His presence,
  From the radiance of His Face—

Christ, the Son of God, hath sent me
  Through the midnight lands;
Mine the mighty ordination
  Of the piercéd Hands.

Mine the message grand and glorious,
  Strange unsealed surprise,—
That the goal is God's beloved,
  Christ in Paradise.

Hear me, weary men and women,
  Sinners dead in sin;
I am come from heaven to tell you
  Of the love within.

.   .   .   .

There, as knit unto the body,
  Every joint and limb,
We, His ransomed, His beloved,
  We are one with Him.

.   .

On into the depths eternal
  Of the love and song,
Where in God the Father's glory
  Christ has waited long;

There to find that none beside Him
God's delight can be—
Not beside Him, nay, but in Him,
O beloved, are we.[1]

I WANT to write the beginning of this chapter to boys and girls. All the young ones were great favourites with Mr. Stewart.

He was so glad when he found the boys and girls taking an interest in God's work among the heathen. He used to say that "C.M.S." stood not only for "Church Missionary Society," but that it meant, too, "Come, Master, Soon," as he felt this to be the true way of hastening His coming and kingdom.

He used to say that the right way to get new missionaries must be the way Christ Himself taught us. He said, "*Pray* ye the Lord of the harvest, that He may send forth labourers into His harvest." This, he said, was as much the Lord's prayer as the prayer that is usually called by that name, and yet how few pray the first "Pray ye" compared to the number who say "Our Father."

How glad he will be if he hears (and I think Christ will tell him—don't you?) that some boys and girls in the United Kingdom and in the Colonies have begun to pray for, and to help, the boys and girls in China, for whom he prayed so earnestly and worked so diligently!

Do not say in a hurry "I can do nothing."

God works *in* those who let Him, "to will and do of His good pleasure."

[1] From "Hymns of Tersteegen and Others," by Mrs. Bevan.

Let me tell you what some children *have* done.

They belong to a Bible Class, and the teacher told them—what I want the children who read this chapter to know—that they could have a school of their own in China for £4 a year.

I suppose some of them thought it would be nicer to help to send the knowledge of Jesus to China than to buy *all* the sweets they had been accustomed to ; but be that as it may, they gave their pennies, and tle kind teacher sent £4. I hope after some time a letter will come from China telling them where their school is, and describing the village, the teacher, and the scholars, so that they can pray as well as send pennies.

If eighteen boys or girls would band themselves together, each giving one penny every week, they could send £4 0s. 8d.—enough for a school, and the 8d. over would pay for postage.

They could choose one to be secretary and another for treasurer, and so have a little Missionary Society of their own.

I am sure they would soon feel the need of prayer ; and they would ask God to fill the Chinese school-master with His Holy Spirit, that he might teach the children and their parents when he visits them all that God wants them to know.

So that it would come to be the missionary children's *village*, not only their *school*.

I remember a story Mr. Stewart told about a Chinese boy he met.

It happened in this way. Mr. Stewart came to a

village where, he was told, there were no Christians except one boy. He asked at a door for a drink of water; he was weary and thirsty. It was only water that he *asked* for; he *got* some information that refreshed his heart.

"Have you ever heard of Jesus Christ?" he asked the woman who came to the door.

"Oh, yes. My boy of twelve years old is always talking about Him. He wants me to give up the idols and burn them, but I dare not do that."

Mr. Stewart started again on his journey, walking in the dust and heat as his Master did, having learned from the mother that the boy had gone up the mountain on some errand.

I forgot to mention one important thing the mother said. After saying she feared to burn the idols, she added: "I sometimes think my son must be right; he is so changed. He used to be selfish and bad-tempered; now he is unselfish and patient, and he says it is Jesus Christ has made the change."

Mr. Stewart had to go across the mountain, and I know not how many steps he had to climb to reach the summit—like a steep flight of stairs.

About half way up he saw a boy coming towards him, descending as he ascended. As he approached Mr. Stewart felt no doubt that this was the one Christian in the village; he recognised in the bright face and fearless eye a brother in Christ.

Great was the joy of the youthful disciple to meet the foreign Singang (teacher).

I cannot tell you all the conversation, but this I do remember: the boy told Mr. Stewart that he had only once heard of Jesus—" the One," as he said, " who loved *me* enough to die for me. And I could not help loving Him with all my heart as soon as ever I heard of Him. I feel now that I could die for Him.

" I had gone to the wedding feast of my cousin, a long journey over the mountain, and there was one Christian there. I heard he had some strange new doctrine he had learned from ' foreign devils.'

" I felt a great desire to hear, and he told me something better than new doctrine. He told me of my Saviour, my Friend, my Lord."

I cannot tell you how much more God taught that dear boy through Mr. Stewart, sitting on the mountain side; and I do not quite remember if a little school was started in that village—I think so. But I know that some time after Mrs. Stewart was visiting at Kucheng (where she afterwards resided). She examined the women in the school there—the Training School for Bible-women—and noticing one woman with a spiritual perception far beyond the others, she spoke to her personally after the Bible lesson. The woman told her where she came from and her name, and she was identified as the mother of this boy.

Mr. Stewart longed to have schools for boys and girls in all the villages.

The following accounts were written by Mr. Stewart as " Reports " for those who contributed to the Day School Fund. We reprint them here, that they may have a wider circulation.

I

REPORT OF THE FUH-KIEN DAY SCHOOLS.

August, 1893.

DEAR FRIENDS,—

Through absence in the Colonies[1] last year, I was unable to send a Report at the usual time, and am now reprinting my article on the School from this month's *Gleaner*. I am returning (D.V.) to Fuh-kien the beginning of September, and my sister, Miss Smyly, 35, Fitzwilliam Street, Dublin, has most kindly promised to receive contributions, and give information.

Some fourteen years ago we in Fuh-kien felt that an attempt should be made to establish Christian schools throughout the country, and on a more distinctly self-supporting basis than had yet been attempted.

We had then about half-a-dozen little schools; but on our stating our intention to in future confine our pecuniary assistance to £4 per school per annum, all above this for all purposes connected with the school, or the salary of the teacher, to be found by the scholars themselves, several of these teachers sent in their resignation.

However, we persevered in our determination, and made it a constant matter of prayer, both in public with the Chinese converts and among ourselves, that if it were God's will He would bless these little schools; and the result was that, to our great delight,

[1] Mr. Stewart visited the Colonies in company with Mr. Eugene Stock.

the demand for them increased, and the number gradually mounted from those first three or four up to ninety-six last year. Our other rules regarding them were, that the *teachers should all of them be converts*, and that the scholars should learn our Christian books, written in the simplest and most direct language by ourselves, treating of the vital doctrines of Christianity, and also of course the Bible, and give half their school-time *each day of the week* to the study of them.

The annual examination of these schools was perhaps the happiest part of my work, and they proved themselves to be an *evangelistic* agency beyond our expectation; for not only was light brought into many dark homes by means of the children, but also many adults came to the schoolmasters to be taught in the evenings when their day's work was done. Also at our examinations crowds of the heathen thronged the room, listening attentively as we catechised the children on the great fundamental doctrines of the true Faith. Of course we took care that these listeners should understand the questions and the answers, and thus we preached to them in perhaps the most effective of all ways.

These ninety-six schools are distributed over an immense tract of country, often five or ten miles, or even more, from one another. Sometimes you find one in a far outlying district, the only centre of Christian light in a wide area of heathenism; and there are places in the Province now, where the thriving little church that exists there owes its origin to the establishment of one of those tiny schools.

Mr. Lloyd, writing some time ago from the district of Hing-hwa, gave a striking illustration of this. A request came to him to establish a Christian school in the village; he did so, and through the instrumentality of the schoolmaster, who was "a very earnest man, with a good influence outside the school," an interest began at once to spring up; this steadily increased, till in the short space of two years the number of converts had grown to 150. He added that the converts had proved the reality of their faith by subscribing liberally towards the erection of a much-needed church, schoolroom, and catechist's house, having given ninety dollars in money, and about 1,500 days' labour, and various gifts of tiles, etc. "It is built," he writes, "of red brick, entirely in the native style of architecture, and as I came in sight of it I could have cried with joy at what God had wrought by His grace in that village. What a joy it was to examine a school in that nice building, knowing as I did, that only two years before the Christians could have been counted on the fingers of one hand, and that, humanly speaking, *but for our little school all would still be in heathen darkness!*"

A good illustration of the usefulness of one of these little day schools in a far outlying district, and the way in which it becomes a centre of Christian instruction to those seeking it, is given by Mr. Collins.

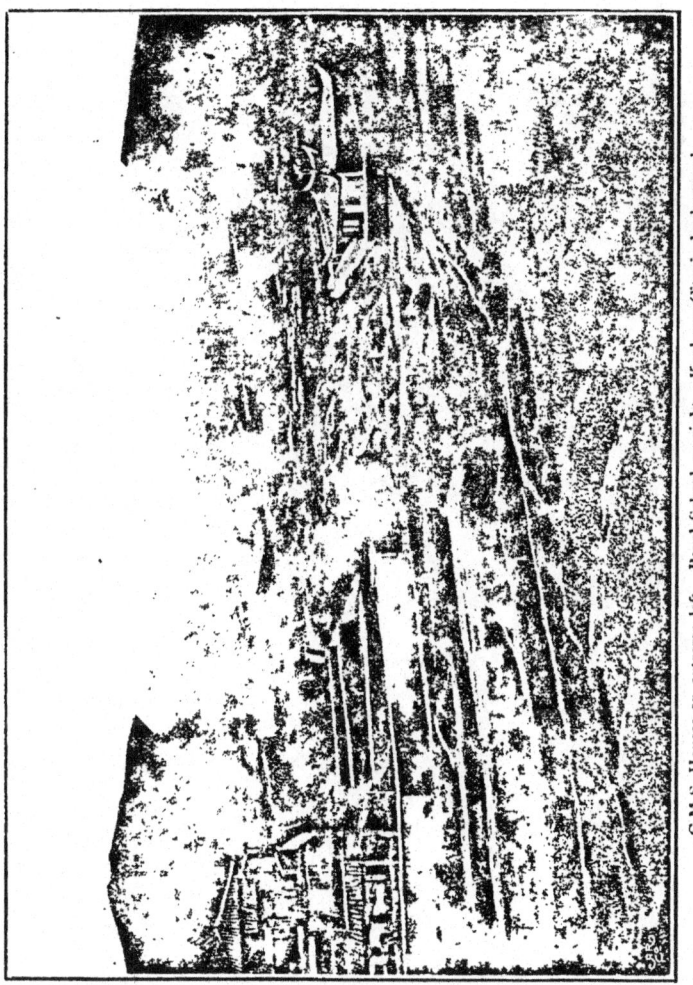

C.M.S. Houses on extreme left. Boys' School on right. Kucheng City in background.

His experience, too, shows how much good may be done on the journey to the school; he writes:—

"'There is a great interest awakened in A-cai,' said the native clergyman to me. 'I went there and stayed two nights and all the village came to listen.' 'Where is A-cai?' I asked, as the name was unfamiliar. 'Down by the sea—it is the village to which the school was moved this year,' he answered. Directly he said that, I remembered that the schoolmaster was a very earnest man, a true Christian, and a keen student of his Bible, and I had been expecting to hear further news of him. I had heard that he had twelve scholars coming to his school every day, and sixteen at night—boys whose work prevented them coming at any other time—so I was heartily glad when I found myself seated in a large boat that sails daily down to the sea-coast villages. There was no limit to the number this boat could contain apparently—to-day it was particularly crowded. As soon as I got on board I was greeted at once by a cheery 'Ping ang' ('Peace to you') from two men, and found that there were two or three Christians on board. The people crowded round me, and I resigned myself to my fate. I knew what was coming, and gave myself up at once to silent prayer, for it is a very real trial for me to be overhauled and mauled by a crowd on a hot June morning, and to answer with perfect equanimity a thousand questions, each more extraordinary than the one before; to have every garment pierced and felt by every hand that

can reach it, and to be catechised on the state of the
tea-market, and the value of a dollar in England.
Presently an old man came and sat down near me,
and in answer to a question as to where he was
going, said, 'To A-cai.' So at once we struck up a
friendly talk. He had heard the Gospel from the
schoolmaster, Mr. Ding, and at once, to my complete
surprise, asked me to read some of it to him, 'As Mr.
D. does every evening.' Out came my Testament,
and the fire of questions ceased as I read St. John
iii. 1–18. I thought this old man promised well for
A-cai.

"A crowd of coolies with their loads joined us from
another boat, and the noise and confusion preventing
conversation, I opened my ink-bottle and letter-case
to write. 'What's he got there—is he eating opium?'
shouted a man who was too far off to see, and took
the pen for a pipe-stem. That gave me an opening,
and they carried away a very distinct idea of what
English Christians out here think of the opium
question. I overhead one man say reflectively to
his friend, some time after, 'He says what they hate
most is opium.'

"Shortly after, another man took the ink for
morphia; for some reason it was connected with
opium in his mind. They then conversed about
foreigners in general, and some of their ideas were
new to me. I gathered that there was a race of
foreigners who were all women, no men! that there
was one kingdom which no ship built with iron nails

could ever get to, and so on. At length I made a last effort, and quoting St. John iii. 12, caught their attention, and with the help of the little 'wordless book,' had a capital time with them.

"A welcome mid-day rest was obtained in the little church at A-ling, and in the afternoon I started for A-cai with the A-ling catechist. He told me how some new enquirers had come over to him, influenced by the A-cai schoolmaster.

"Leaving the coast, we began slowly to ascend the steep little range of hills. Once at the top, we saw before us a narrow glen, with steep rocky sides that even these industrious Chinese could not cultivate, and beyond it another range of hills, bare, rocky, and precipitous, with scarcely a tree to be seen. One, indeed, there was, at the hill foot on the opposite side of the glen, a tree that has a history of its own. Further along the shore is a farm-house, owned by a man who has been long a Christian. He held to his faith stoutly in spite of bitter persecution, and Sunday by Sunday came along this lonely glen on his way to church. One Sunday a party of opium smokers lay in wait for him, caught him and tied him to this tree, and cruelly beating him, left him there. But the beating had not the desired effect, for he still continued to go to church. Then his heathen neighbours seized some of his land and the trees planted on it. Having full proof of legal possession, he took the case to the law court; but the mandarin was no friend to the Christians, and gave the man his choice between imprisonment and freedom, but the latter only on condition that he burnt incense before an idol. This he refused to do, and chose the prison.

"As we passed round the corner of the cliff that shuts in the glen, there opened to our view a beautiful little cove, that reminded one of Devonshire, and the likeness increased as the tide came in and covered the mud flats. Skirting the foot of the hills, we followed the path to the right of the little bay, and turning another corner came suddenly on the place we sought, the village of A-cai.

"This was the first time a foreigner had been there, and the news soon spread. The first old man we met, holding up both hands in astonishment, exclaimed, 'Why, some of them arrive at the age of fifty or sixty years, do they?' This was a compliment to my supposed grey hair! He was more dumbfounded still to hear I was only thirty. The villagers treated us with marked courtesy, and not once did one hear an objectionable expression. Politeness like this is not unusual in remote places away from the high roads.

"The sun was setting behind the mountains, and the cool sea breeze which the incoming tide brought with it made a welcome change after the hot day. The little schoolroom, evidently once a shop, was densely crowded, so they placed a table outside the house, with a lantern on it, and the preaching began. It was a thoroughly Chinese scene, the audience sat on doorsteps, window-sills, benches and chairs, and on the low wall that bounded the little terrace were sixteen children, evidently the night-school. The sky was dark, and only the stars lighted the scene, if we except our flickering candle. I began with a few words, but gave way to the schoolmaster. He spoke well and to the point, the audience interrupting freely with questions, some showing earnest thought, and none of the flippant mocking questions so usual in street preaching. Only half-a-dozen of the foremost men could be seen in the light, but every now and then a voice would come out of the gloom, or a smart discussion would spring up resembling a duel, and sounding not unlike a quarrel to unaccustomed ears. Then the preacher would go back to his subject and silence would reign.

"As the catechist preached, suddenly two men shouted out, ' Then the worship of idols is useless,' and a tumult of voices arose which ceased as suddenly, while he gave a clear and decided answer.

"Meanwhile the schoolmaster was not idle. He had gone into the schoolroom, which was full of people who preferred a seat in the light, with a pipe and a cup of tea, and there was holding an animated discussion on some subject of which I could catch only a word now and then.

"Looking in from the darkness, one could only judge from the shadows on the mud wall thrown by the light that the argument was a hot one, it looked once or twice as if more than moral persuasion was being resorted to, but it was all perfectly good-natured.

" The catechist's voice failing, my load-bearer, a fine old Christian, came to the rescue, and his rough voice broke the silence, evidently making some telling points, which the audience much appreciated. The old charges that the missionaries take people's eyes and knee-caps to make medicine of were brought forward, and talking continued for over three hours. It must have been quite eleven o'clock before the last man went off and the Christians had prayers.

" To me this was the most interesting evening I had spent since landing in China. The courtesy of the people and their earnestness, with the evident spirit of real inquiry that they showed, made me most hopeful for the future. The schoolmaster's humility and reality mark him as a man whom God the Holy Ghost can use.

" I talked to the children at prayers the next day, and found them very bright and intelligent, and well up in the main facts of the Gospel story. Surely it is a cause of great thankfulness that thirty little ones should be learning something of the way of life at that little country day school. It is our best school in that district, but what one is all may be in time, and they will prove no mean instruments in freeing this enslaved people from the bondage of Satan."

Of the schools in the wide district south of Foochow, far removed from the district just spoken of, Mr. Lloyd gives some very interesting particulars:—

" *Chia-yang.*—At the beginning of the year we started a school in this village at the request of a man who had heard the Gospel at Sieng-iu, and had walked ten miles to Sunday service for some months. He had induced some eight or ten of his neighbours to join him in petitioning us to send them a teacher, and assured us that numbers of the people were anxious to hear about the 'Religion of Jesus.' The result has surpassed our most sanguine expectations. I visited the village some weeks since, and was both pleased and surprised to find some eighty persons assembled to meet me with every token of respect, all of whom had enrolled their names as desirous to serve Christ and forsake their idols. Two old men especially attracted my attention. One of them, a village elder, very old and feeble, hobbled to the school, and was with great difficulty prevented kneeling down to me; he insisted that he wished thus to honour me as the representative of Christ, and was a little displeased when we pointed out that it must not be. Will not the supporters of our day schools sometimes think of this little company of disciples in this remote mountain village, nestling among the hills 3,000 feet above the sea level, and pray that the little school may be a centre of light to the whole neighbourhood?

" *Eng-tau-kiang*.—Our attempt to open a school at this village two years ago met with such violent opposition that we were obliged, perforce, to close it. Two of our ' voluntary exhorters,' who went thither and endeavoured to quell the disturbance, were bespattered with unmentionable filth, and sent whence they came. This year the attitude of the people has quite changed and sixty or seventy of them are attending the Sunday services. The schoolmaster is allowed to carry on his work unmolested, and we are deeply thankful that animosity has given way to glad acceptance on the part of many."

Here is one other illustration of the good work these little schools are doing, also from Mr. Lloyd :—

" *Leng-tie.*—This village is situated in the Sieng-iu plain, about three miles from the city. I am glad to say that the establishment of the school has led to an increased interest in Christianity, and some ten of the villagers have joined us. One man among these recent converts attracted my attention at once, as being evidently in good circumstances, and quite above the majority of the people. I had a long conversation with him, and we read the New Testament together. He seems really sincere, and I do trust his influence may be felt."

These cases show, I think, what valuable work these day schools are doing, not only in reaching the children, but bringing the Gospel message to their adult friends as well, and the faster we can scatter them through the length and breadth of the country, the sooner will it be evangelized. The small amount of help, too, that comes from outside sources for their maintenance, £4 per annum, as I mentioned above, tends to foster a spirit of independence and self-support. Why the heathen priests and literati allow the children—for most of them are from *heathen* homes—to attend and learn our Christian books, it is hard to understand, except that, in answer to the prayers of those supporting these little schools, God is graciously protecting them and blessing them. Out of the ninety-six only fourteen are paid from the C.M.S. general funds; the rest are supported privately, and this means a good number of true friends specially interested in this work, and whose prayers are being abundantly answered.

Yours very sincerely,

ROBERT W. STEWART.

The Rev. R. W. Stewart writes from Kucheng :—

"At the beginning of the year, at our native Conference, when the leading native Christians from all parts of my two districts of Kucheng and Pingnang came together for four days' consultation and Christian intercourse, requests were handed in from twenty-eight new places for schools. Each application gave the names of those who would attend the school, and the amount they were willing to subscribe to add to our £4 for the teacher's salary. I believe so thoroughly in these little schools that I could not refuse them, and so they were allowed, and I am trusting for the needful funds. These 28 new schools in my own district, added to some new ones in other districts, bring up the number to over 90. So you will believe that some new subscribers' names on your list was a pleasant sight, and if the old friends will stand firm, we shall get along without coming into the bankruptcy court. I have not the least fear

of this, for if it be of God, it will not fail, and if it
be not of God, I hope it will fail."

"The good point about these country schools is that
they are distinctly 'Evangelistic' in character. I
have examined them once this year, and find that
6 or 7 out of every 10 come from heathen homes,
utterly heathen, the adult members of the house never
going near church or chapel. The children, however,
come, and every day read our Christian books. I
examined them in nothing else, and I am sure that
what they learn in that way, and learn thoroughly,
will bring forth fruit one day. But it is bringing
forth fruit already here and there. In more than one
place, where there is now a native church, a few
years ago there was only one of these schools, and
the work began from that, so that friends at home
who are making it possible to carry on these little
schools are as really 'Evangelizing China' as any of
us out here."

The following is a translation of a letter written
by Li Daih-ching, who is the teacher at the school at
Dong-kio, to the Rev. T. M'Clelland:—

"Teacher M'Clelland, peace! I have been appointed
to Dong-kio. I have myself no good method of accomplishing my work, and hope you will always by
prayer help me. I hope God will give me His Holy
Spirit, and show me the right way to teach my
scholars, that they may know God. At Dong-kio at
present 60 or 70 regularly come to worship on Sunday. Sometimes many more come. There are some

whose faith is 'great,' and some whose faith is 'small.' My school is as far from the chapel as the Foochow boys' school is from the college. More I cannot write. Greeting to the Teacher's Lady."

"KUCHENG, FOOCHOW, *January* 23, 1895.

" DEAR FRIENDS,—

" I am extremely grateful to you for helping us again this year, by providing so large a number of Christian Day Schools throughout the country.

" On returning to China after my furlough, a year ago, I found I had been appointed to take charge of the two inland districts, or, as we would call them in England, 'counties,' of Kucheng and Ping-nang, covering an area equal to about half the size of Wales.

" At our first native Conference, which was held the beginning of February, applications came in from all directions for these Christian Day Schools. Each application gave the number of scholars promising to attend, and the amount of money they would sub-scribe, the assistance from foreign sources being, as you know, limited to £4 per annum for *everything* connected with the school.

" On reckoning up the number applied for, and finding that it meant an increase of 28 over the pre-vious year, I hesitated, wondering if funds would come in sufficient, but the hesitation was not very long. If they were of God, He would send the funds ; if they were not, then we would take that as a sign.

K

We prayed about it, and gave consent. Sufficient funds *have* come in, and we regard it as a proof that they have God's approval, and heartily thank those through whom He has sent it.

"I have just returned from a long school-inspecting tour through my two great districts, and have been surprised at the improvement everywhere visible, over the last time I went round, before going home to England. Not only were the Christian books learned thoroughly by heart, so that again and again nine children out of ten got full marks, but also, what I felt still more glad about, there was a clear grasp of the fundamental truths of Christianity and the way of salvation.

"Crowds of heathen came in to listen, and stood perfectly still for sometimes two hours, and even on to three hours, while I catechised the children on the entrance of sin into the world, the need for a Saviour, His love and death for us, and our life of service for Him now. This is, I feel sure, the most effective kind of preaching to the heathen, and would be worth all the trouble and expense, even if it were no gain at all to the children. It is the most powerful agency for *evangelizing* the country that we have.

"You may ask, 'What signs are there of this?' I am glad to say there are many. In place after place, I found that the adults joining the church were preceded by their children joining the school. Out of the 58 schools in my districts, 31 are in places where there are *no other Christian teachers*, and in a good number of these I found great interest excited in the village, and a small congregation on Sunday ministered to by the schoolmaster ; indeed, I felt that the interest circling round the schools was as great as where catechists were placed.

" The individual instances of adult friends being brought in by the children were very encouraging, and far too many to enter here. One little girl was the means of leading seven members of her house to worship ; another had brought in her father, mother, and grandfather, etc., etc.

" One of our C.E.Z.M.S. sisters tells me of a case she came on in the western part of this district. ' At the beginning of 1894, there was a Day School started at Siong-ngiang, and one of the first scholars was a little girl called Geng-sai. She eagerly learned, going home and telling as much as she could about the Jesus she loved. Her home people seeing how earnest and real she was, began to think it would be a good thing for them if they went to church ; and so began to go and worship God, and hear for themselves. Now the whole household worships God, and in October they invited the catechist, and other Christians, to come to their house, when they collected all the idols together and burned them (seven or eight in number), putting up in their place the Ten Commandments.' "

" The same lady tells of another place where a woman specially attracted her attention by her knowledge of the true God, and her desire to know more. This was through her little boy, for 'in this place there is no one to teach the women,' and so this woman only knows what the little boy has come home and told her. She eagerly learned a little prayer to repeat every day, and said she would worship God.

"So far I have only spoken of my own two districts in the centre of the Province, but your schools are scattered over a still wider region. From the far North-East, in the Fuh-ning Prefecture, Mr. Eyton Jones writes, 'On behalf of our Fuh-ning Church, I must send through you to the friends at home sincere thanks for your assistance in starting four Day Schools. The school at Sing-sang fishing hamlet has been useful, not only in getting a few little ones together, but for the strengthening of the adults, whom the teacher assembles for evening prayers. One of the little lads has been the means of bringing in his father.'

"South of the last-named Prefecture lie the districts of Ning-taik and Lo-nguong, and scattered through these you have the goodly number of twenty-three schools. Mr. Martin, the missionary in charge, writes: 'These schools have given us more satisfaction the last two years; they are better attended, and in some villages the schoolmasters teach also catechumens and Christians, and in all the villages where we have schools these masters preach Jesus, and are lights in centres of gross darkness. I have had applications from heathen to open schools, and to send

Christian teachers, the reason given being, in your schools you teach the children to speak the truth, to obey their parents, and to give up bad habits!'

"South of Foochow and the river Min, you have, through the districts of Hok-chiang, Hing-hwa, and Sieng-iu, over thirty schools. The missionaries in charge give good reports of them all. A C.E.Z. lady gives interesting particulars of those round her station of Dang-seng :—

"'Although my work is not among the little boys of our day schools, I should like to say what a very great help these schools are to the evangelistic work carried on in our district.

"'I am stationed at Dang-seng, and within about eight miles radius we have had ten boys' day schools open during the past year. The attendance varies of course, but generally we have twenty-five children; in our largest schools, thirty-five and more.

"'In visiting a village I generally go first to the school; after a little talk there, we go outside the building, and find the news has spread, and quite a good number are waiting to hear the Gospel message. In this way the school becomes an introduction for an open-air meeting. If many follow me into the building, I take one of the school-books, and question the children on the important truths of our religion— the Creation, the work of our Saviour, His blessed coming again, the folly of idols, and so on; watching our hearers to see what they can understand, and explaining the meaning of our questions.

" ' Then again, it is a great joy to me to see progress in the teachers themselves. There are three men now teaching, who two years ago were dark heathen; they attended our services, learned the way of salvation, and when it was seen the work was real, were put into their posts. In some cases, particularly, I can see how they are growing in the knowledge of our Saviour. Three weeks ago, I heard one of these preach at Dang-seng, on Sunday morning. He was very nervous, and preached a short sermon; but it was earnest and thoughtful, and one could see how by constant teaching he had really grasped the truths he sought to teach the little boys.

" ' Then again, a fortnight ago, we were asking who wished to be prepared for baptism, and amongst others was one of our former scholars, a lad of sixteen or seventeen years. He used to come to our little school at Dang-seng, then went to work in the fields, but came to evening prayers and the Sunday services; now we find him wanting to take a stand and publicly confess Christ by baptism.

" ' Another younger lad, also a former scholar, is asking for baptism at the new year. The seed has been sown in early childhood, and being the good seed of the Word of God, it will certainly spring up, and bring forth fruit.

" ' In four of our village schools, there is a regular Sunday morning service at which Christian men and women, from that and neighbouring villages, gather to worship God. One must not limit the influence of these schools; each one can be, and by the power of God shall I believe be, a light in a dark place, and the means of bringing many little ones to the feet of our Saviour.

" ' I forgot to say that, during the past year, I had a weekly Bible-class with the teachers of our schools. We study the Gospel of St. Mark for two hours each Wednesday. I gave them written papers to take home and answer, and found that in this way our lesson was well remembered.'

" Let me in conclusion repeat the three fundamental rules which guide us :—

" (1) The scholars must all read daily our Christian books, and pass examinations in them several times in the year.

" (2) The teachers must all be baptized converts.

" (3) The amount of foreign aid towards the entire support of the school, renting the room, books, and furniture, as well as the teacher's salary, must not exceed £4 per annum.

" On the sum you put into my hands last year, we had 119 schools, an increase of more than 30 on the previous year. In this coming year I hope we shall be able to keep up at least as many, and perhaps add a few.

" Let me beg of you to remember these little schools in your prayers as often as you can. The success that has so far attended them is, I firmly believe, due more to that than to any other cause.

" Yours very sincerely,

" ROBERT W. STEWART."

"Since writing the above, Mr. Shaw, who is in charge of Hing-hwa, the most southerly of our districts, writes: 'I wonder if you could let us open three more schools down here. I am thankful to say there are wonderful openings, and it would be such a blessing if we could get these schools.'"

"To this I have at once replied, 'Yes.'"

Mrs. Stewart wrote to the lady who is head of the Missionary House in Dublin for the Agents of the Irish Church Missions and Dublin Visiting Mission :—

"I hear the inhabitants of your House have subscribed £4 for one of our day schools in this province. Will you please convey to them our warmest thanks? But we trust that something far better than thanks will be their reward, if they will help by prayer also— even boys and girls saved from the power of sin and Satan to be their crown of rejoicing by-and-by.

"We feel more and more convinced since our return to China this time that these schools are perhaps the best means of 'evangelizing' the country.

"A schoolmaster in China is always acceptable ; and a school can be started in some new place when a catechist would not be allowed to enter, and a foreigner would not be listened to.

.   .   .   .   .

"In these two districts there are now fifty day schools,—twice as many as last year.

"We felt sure when these new schools were asked for, that it must be the Lord's will . . . And though we had not got the needed money, Mr. Stewart gave leave to open them, for we had asked the Lord to send the money. . . .

" Your House will now be the means of supporting one of these schools, and we have heard of several others being undertaken.

" Mr. Stewart was much pleased with the way the children answered the last time he examined some of the schools. They are scattered over a wide district. The two districts of Kucheng and Ping-nang are larger than half of Wales, with a greater population.

" You can imagine the difficulty of .superintending such a work, with no railways, or even carriages ! "

And now the schools and schoolmasters have lost their superintendent. God has another way for him to work now.

But we trust that the little schools will go on. The Chinese schoolmasters will be called to greater earnestness and diligence through the trial which has come to them. The friends who have prayed for the children, and given the necessary £4 a year for each school, will have a chastened joy now in seeing to it that the work shall not be left to languish for want of supplies from the home-land.

If God has touched hearts through the recital of China's needs, let us be practical. When God so loved the world He proved it by *giving* His only Son.

If we love God, and love to spread the knowledge that " Jesus saves," let us ask ourselves—-may God

ask us—if we are letting Him use us, use our money,
all we have and all we are, just as He pleases, that
God in all things may be glorified through Jesus
Christ.

CHAPTER VI

CHRIST MAGNIFIED

"According to my earnest expectation and my hope, that . . . Christ shall be magnified in my body, whether it be by life or by death."—PHIL. i. 20.

CHAPTER VI

CHRIST MAGNIFIED

2 SAM. xv. 19-22.   JOHN xii. 26.

"Wherefore goest thou with Me?"
   Said the King disowned—
Said the King despised, rejected,
   Disenthroned.

     .   .   .   .

"As the Lord lives and the King,
   Ever Lord to me,
Where in death or life He dwelleth
   I will be."

"Go—pass over," spake the King;
   Then passed Ittai o'er;
Passed into the place of exile
   From the shore.

     .   .   .   .

"Go—pass over"; words of grace,
   Spoken, Lord, to me,
That, in death or life, where Thou art
   I might be.

     .   .   .   .

Hidden there with Christ in God,
   That blest life I share :
Christ it is who liveth in me—
   Liveth there.

"He who serves me," spake His lips,
   "Let him follow Me ;
And where I am shall My servant
   Ever be."

Follow, where His steps lead on,
  Through the golden street ;
Far into the depths of glory
  Track His feet.

Till unto the throne of God,
  Of the Lamb I come ;
There to share the blessed welcome,
  Welcome home !

There with Him whom man rejected,
  In the light above,
Those whom God, His Father, honours,
  Such His love.

                              P. G.[1]

PHILIPPIANS i. 20, was the text Louisa Stewart wrote in a copy of " Daily Light " given by her to a sister before her first journey to China, in 1876. A friend writes :—

" When I first read the telegram, words that I had heard Mrs. Stewart say at a meeting came rushing into my mind with such force, something like this,— ' If it should ever be that we meet our deaths by violence, let no one think that God has in any way failed us. We are nowhere promised that His servants may not be called upon to suffer, even to *die* for *His* sake, who died for us.

" What we *are* promised is that, living or dying, we cannot be separated from Him; and that under all circumstances He will be sufficient."

Yes, that was indeed the deep undertone of both their lives—living or dying, they were the Lord's.

" The sting of death is sin." And our Saviour Jesus

---

[1] In " Hymns of Tersteegen and Others," by Frances Bevan.

Christ "put away sin by the sacrifice of Himself."
He has " abolished death, and brought life and immor-
tality to light through the Gospel."

An old friend writes, one who knew Louisa Stewart
from her early childhood :—

" I well remember dear Louisa's remark to me when
I regretfully bid her farewell before her marriage, as
I was leaving home.

" She said she had some time before given herself to
God, that He might use her in whatever way or place
He pleased. Therefore she felt sure His Hand was
guiding her, and her sole desire was that His Will
should be done in and by her, and that Christ should
be magnified in her body, whether by life or death.

" Her beautiful simplicity of character, her self-
forgetfulness and unobtrusiveness were remarkable,
even in early years.

" Many took notice of the extreme simplicity and
earnestness with which she spoke at the *enormous*
meeting at the Pavilion, Brighton, four years ago,
when Mrs. Ahok was with her.

" The interpretation was so clearly spoken, and in
her usual quiet voice, yet she was heard at the farthest
end. Many remarked afterwards with what ease she
interpreted each sentence as Mrs. Ahok spoke. She is
still remembered in Brighton.

" One loves to think of her, and to praise God for
what He accomplished through her, weak in herself,
yet strong *in the LORD*."

I hesitated as to reprinting some of the loving words
knowing how they both shrank from being praised.

One of the children said, when shown a letter in which his father was highly spoken of, " Father never liked to be praised " ; and this was equally true of his wife.   They had been baptized into the same Spirit— the Spirit of Jesus Christ.   Wherever we find His spirit, in man, woman, or child, it is ever humble and teachable—the spirit of the little child.

A story is told of the early English Church, when first the Bishop of Rome sent a legate to this country. Those who had been appointed as the deputation to receive him went to seek advice of a " saint," who lived apart with God.

" How shall we know," they questioned, " if he is a true servant of God, and sent by Him ? "

The saint answered : " My children, if you find him humble, meek and lowly, like Jesus Christ, then know that he has indeed come among us a true messenger from God.

" But if you find him proud and self-conceited, if he proudly keeps his seat, and does not rise to his feet to receive you, then know that he is no true servant of God.   For ' The proud He knoweth afar off.' "

If the Chinese had known of this simple test, I think they would have judged that Robert and Louisa Stewart were true followers of Jesus Christ.   Not their *own* humility, but that of the Christ who lived in them. They had both learned that simple yet deep theology— revealed by God Himself to the babes ; hidden (solemn word !) by God the Father from the wise and prudent— contained in the Apostle Paul's simple testimony, " Not I, but Christ liveth in me."

Not only—though *that* they also said—"I laboured
. . . yet not I, but the grace of God was with me,"
but, in true humility, ascribing the very *life* to Him,
so that in all things, great and small, it is "*Not I,*
but *Christ.*" Simple creed, contained in four words!
Beautiful life, dependent on the "root and fatness" of
the tree; for if the root be holy, so are the branches!

"I am the Vine, ye are the branches," said our
Saviour Jesus Christ.

" Abide in Me, and I in you."

Oh, wonderful love, that cannot be satisfied until
those who once were lost in sin are not only made
nigh through the blood of Christ, but brought into
such union that they share His very Life.

Only one Life, and that Christ's Life.

"I no longer live, but Christ liveth in me " (Gal. ii.
20, R.V., margin).

Dr. Van Someren Taylor's account of Robert and
Louisa Stewart, published in *The Life of Faith*; and in
the same paper (a week later) : " Some Recollections of
Mrs. Stewart," we feel ought to be preserved. Dr.
Taylor was an intimate friend, and he and Mrs. Taylor
were fellow-labourers with Mr. and Mrs. Stewart.

Robert Warren Stewart and Louisa Stewart.

To the readers of *The Life of Faith*, the names of
Robert and Louisa Stewart must be well known, and
now that God has called them home to Himself, and
their names are added to " the noble army of martyrs,"
a few lines from one who knew them so well may be
welcome.   L

To some it is given to follow Christ through the quiet pasture-field, where all is smooth and pleasant. To others it is given to follow the path which lies over the rugged rock, covered with briars and brambles: it was to such a life God called those who have laid down their lives for Him.

As an honour man of T.C.D., Robert Stewart had every prospect of making a name and position in the world. But this, together with a luxurious home, he gave up to become a poor missionary.

I remember he told me that a Chinaman once said to him, " I know why you have become a missionary." " Why ? " asked Stewart. The Chinaman's reply was significant. Forming one hand into the shape of a bowl of rice, with the other he worked as if he were holding chop-sticks and cramming rice into his mouth, meaning thereby, " To obtain food to eat." How well do I remember Stewart's comment to me on it; it was, " He little knew." Years afterwards, as I saw him at his father's beautiful house in Ireland, I well understood what, from an earthly point of view, it must have cost Stewart to go to a foreign field ; but never did I hear him speak of "giving up" or "hardship." To him a missionary's calling was the noblest calling on earth, and he regarded it as a privilege and an honour to be engaged in it.

Soon after he arrived in China he was placed in charge of the educational work of the Mission, and it was as an educational missionary I knew him. Through his efforts funds were raised for a college (which was afterwards burnt by a Chinese mob), and

his whole time was given up to his students and
scholars.

It was his wish that they should find in him their
friend. He was no distant head, a great personage far
above them. No; as their equal he strove to know
each one personally and individually. He endeavoured
to find out what was the real spiritual life of each one
—what really was their aim in becoming theological
students. Was it really love to Christ and to their
fellow-countrymen; or was it merely to get so many
dollars out of the Church? When he felt a man was
not fitted for the work he did not hesitate to say so,
though by so doing he knew he was drawing down
upon himself odium from others. How often have
I heard him say, " One bad man may do an amount of
harm that three good ones cannot counteract." He
was most anxious that only fit and proper men should
go out as Christian workers amongst their countrymen. On him the glory of large numbers had no
power. " Better no men than bad men," " Better a
few good true men than many bad," was always
before him.

Another thing that was characteristic of him was,
that he was always ready to listen to the Chinaman,
whether he were a student or a poor village Christian.
No matter what he was doing, no matter how tired he
was, he would lay down his pen or book, invite his
guest to be seated, and give himself up to him. No
wonder that by so doing he won his way to many
a heart, and got to know the Chinese character well.
And know it well he did; and this the Chinamen

knew too. They were perfectly aware that he was
not a man to be deceived.

Another point about him was the great sacredness
with which he regarded foreign money. He knew
with what self-denial such money was given at home,
and therefore he was most careful in the expenditure
of foreign funds; and the more so because he felt that,
if a true native church was to be founded, it was not to
be founded on foreign money. He was all the more careful of this lest men should be led to offer for Christian
work with the hope of getting money from the foreigner.

He realized most fully that, as a Christian missionary, his life as well as his mouth must speak; that
what he had to say to others was "Come," not "Go."
He never instructed a Chinaman to do what he was
not prepared to do himself; and I know that one
reason why he stuck to his post to the last was, that
he might by his presence and example cheer and support the Christians in their hour of persecution, and
be found standing at their side ready to bear with
them whatever might befall; and "he has laid down
his life for his sheep."

How well do I remember how his heart's wish was
"to be used of God." How he used to end up the grace
before his meals (which grace was no mere form, but
a real prayer) with these words, "And use us." To
be a "vessel fit for his Master's use" was his longing.

Any one who came in contact with Robert Stewart
will have experienced that strong personal power
that he had over others—a power that arose from his
strong yet humble character. One was conscious that

he was side by side with a man wholly given up to
God; and as he grew in years he grew in grace, and
in greater likeness to Jesus Christ.

By many a chastisement from a Father's loving
hand, by the bitter fire of affliction—how bitter some
who knew him intimately were aware—he was purified.
And now that Master, whom he loved so much and
longed so much to see, has taken him home to Himself.
He has given him what he longed for, a martyr's crown.

Some Recollections of Mrs. Stewart.

Though almost seventeen years have elapsed since
first I met Mrs. Stewart, it seems but as yesterday.
It was late at night. Following Mr. Stewart, I had
walked from the Foreign Settlement into the city of
Foochow. All was new to me. I was tired, and wondering wherever I was being taken to. All I could
do was to follow the form of Stewart in front of me.

Suddenly he stopped and knocked; quickly the door
was opened. The darkness was broken by a flood of
light, and in the midst of the light, surrounded by the
doorway as a frame, stood Mrs. Stewart, her baby on
her arm, holding out her hand to welcome us, her
face beaming with kindness.

Though we were perfect strangers, she took us to
her home and to her heart, ever binding us to her and
to her husband by ties of kindness upon kindness.
We were always welcome, never in the way. To us
always her house was our home when in Foochow,
and it always had a home-like feel about it.

All her life she had been subject to fearful headaches, which might have debarred her from taking up mission work in an energetic manner; but it by no means did so. She threw all her energy into acquiring the language and spoke it beautifully, like a native.

Her first object was to gather around her a few native women, whom she might teach to be teachers of their fellow-countrywomen, teaching them to read and understand their Bibles But Mrs. Stewart by no means confined her attention to those who were to be paid teachers. She welcomed any women who were willing to come (provided she was satisfied that they were fit for admission), and taught them, though in all probability they would simply return to their own homes, there to be unpaid centres of light. She began with three, though the number afterwards increased.

It has been my wife's privilege to have had associated with her one of these women, and we can testify to the thoroughness of her training. How often has she told us, "Mrs. Stewart said so-and-so."

How well can I recall Mrs. Stewart's patience, forbearance, and tact with these women! How patiently she would sit down and listen to their little grievances, sympathizing with them, or kindly rebuking where necessary! Calmly and quietly, never losing her temper, she would talk with the distressed till their angry or ruffled look would vanish, and they would go away comforted and quieted.

This women's work always was regarded as Mrs. Stewart's special work. The funds for it came chiefly, if not almost entirely, from her friends, and through her letters home.

A Bible-women's house was erected, and the number of Bible-women greatly increased. Other ladies were sent out from England, and now at Foochow, Kucheng, Hing-hwa, Sieng-iu, Lo-nguong, we have Bible-women's Training Homes, sending out Bible-women into the surrounding districts. They are worked by foreign ladies of the C.E.Z.M.S and C.M.S.

Mrs. Stewart fully realized that in training these Bible-women one great obstacle was the Chinese written character. It was a great task for these poor, uneducated women to be taught to learn off page after page of Chinese characters, which on their return home they might possibly forget. She therefore adopted the plan of teaching them the system of "Romanized Colloquial," in which Roman letters are used to represent the Chinese sounds. And not merely was this found useful for teaching them to read, but also to write; so that when the women had been trained they might themselves be able to correspond with Mrs. Stewart.

And now we have (thanks to the kind help of the British and Foreign Bible Society) the whole of the New Testament in Romanized Colloquial; and I know much of the work of seeing it through the press in England fell on Mrs. Stewart.

Those who knew her knew how she had always something on hand to extend work amongst the women. Her aim was, as she once wrote to me, and often said, "We must not rest satisfied till every village in China has a Bible-woman in it."

Energetic as she was as a Christian worker, she

never forgot she was a wife, a mother, a hostess. Always at the side of her husband, she helped him in everything. She used often to write letters, and, I think, sermons, at his dictation; and many a weary hour she saved her husband by answering letters for him.

How vividly one can recall that fond, proud look with which she regarded him; and how she understood his every look! How her own face would cloud when she saw him perplexed! And as a mother how tenderly she looked after her little ones, nursing them through more than one serious illness! With what pride she spoke of her sons at home! And as a hostess, too, she was most kind, always looking after every little comfort for those who were her guests.

I cannot finish this short sketch without emphasizing how real was the coming of Christ to her, and that He was to come soon. It seemed always in her thoughts, her calculations—" He is coming very soon." Whilst it stimulated her to greater energy, it yet caused a peaceful calm, a freedom from anxiety, to run through all. Like a true hero, she has fallen at her post, and the call comes to us all to carry on the work that she has left. May each one put to herself the question, " Does God call me ? "

B. VAN SOMEREN TAYLOR, M.B

One subject touched upon by Dr. Taylor, and more fully brought out in the following letters from Dr. Wright (of the Bible Society), and Mr. Stewart's letter addressed to him, is the new method of printing the Bible in Chinese, called the "Romanized" version of the Bible.

Perhaps I shall be only explaining what everybody knows, in saying that *the* great difficulty in the way of the Chinese people learning to read their own language is the Chinese character.

To those who do *not* already know, let me say, a character in Chinese does *not* mean a letter, but each character stands for a *word*.

Originally these characters were pictures, and some of them were amusing.

I remember being told that the Chinese way of representing "peace," is by a picture of a woman being extinguished!

But these pictures, amusing or instructive as the case may have been, are now mere signs, so like each other, and yet different in some small particular, that it is very difficult to carry the difference in the memory. Yet each one represents a different word, so that to read a book, the Bible for example, in Chinese, means that you know every character used in the book. Of course, the same word recurring, you have the same sign, but for each different word there is a different sign.

Now let us fancy these women, who, before coming to the foreign Singsang Iong (Singsang means teacher, Iong his wife), had never learnt anything but to beautify their persons and embroider their tiny shoes. Imagine them having to learn these mysterious signs! No wonder their teachers had to tell of sighs and tears of discouragement.

A friend has sent me an old letter, written by dear Louisa soon after her arrival in China :

"Mr. —— is getting on so fast learning the characters ; he has such a good memory.

"Learning the characters seems to depend purely on memory, Even the characters that I think I know as well as possible I quite forget, unless I keep going over them continually. It is very monotonous work too, and it is hard sometimes not to feel quite tired of it. The servants begin to understand me, but sometimes the man-cook looks surprised and amused, and then I discover that I have been telling him to put carrots in the pudding when I thought I was saying raisins. And another day, I thought I was assuring him that in England we put sugar in our puddings, and found out I had said *soap* instead of sugar. The word is the same ; the tone you say it in makes the difference. Every syllable has seven tones."

This letter was written eighteen years ago.

But the tones were a difficulty to be overcome by the foreigner.

The characters were a real difficulty to their dear native pupils.

The following letters will further explain the importance of the introduction of the Romanized system of writing Chinese.

As Dr. Wright says :—

"Through Mr. Stewart's labours and enthusiasm the New Testament was published in Roman character in the Foochow vernacular."

The practical difference is that now their pupils (men

or women) learn to read the New Testament in three months, instead of the tedious business of former days.

We have received the following correspondence from the British and Foreign Bible Society:

To the Editor of the Daily News.

146, Queen Victoria Street, London, E.C.,

Sir,— *August* 6, 1895.

The first letter I opened this morning was from the murdered missionary, the Rev. R. W. Stewart, and as it shows him peacefully at work for the good of his murderers, it will be read with deep interest by many. Through Mr. Stewart's labours and enthusiasm the New Testament was published in Roman character in the Foochow vernacular. The version was to a certain extent tentative, but its usefulness is now fully established, and Mr. Stewart in his letter pleads for the publication of a similar version in another vernacular. Your readers will notice how earnestly he pleads—and I am sure that my Committee will publish the version as the most effective weapon against such awful outbreaks as that which has now brought sorrow to so many homes. Mr. Stewart was one of the strong men in China, but he was gentle and compassionate as well as strong. He was surrounded by a band of gentle and devoted ladies. On them the blow has fallen. It will be the duty of our Government to take measures against such barbarous outbreaks,—but it is for us to remember that these misguided Chinamen never knew a God who was not as cruel as themselves, and to redouble our efforts that the Gospel of Love may be made a power among them.

I am, Sir, yours faithfully,

W. WRIGHT, D.D.

KUCHENG, FOOCHOW, *June* 24, 1895.

MY DEAR DR. WRIGHT,—

You are exceedingly kind offering to print more for us in Foochow. Romanized Colloquial has not been acknowledged sooner because I was waiting for particulars to enable me to make another request on behalf of another of our dialects, that spoken through a large portion of the great North West Prefecture of Kiong-ning. But, before making my petition, I must say a word on the success of the system in this dialect. I always believed in it, and sixteen years ago stood pretty well alone in the matter, and yet I can truly say that the success that we are now seeing surpasses my expectations. The enclosed memo. has this moment been handed to me by a Z.M.S. lady, who has just come in from the country station of Sa-long, and as I myself examined that very class a month ago, I can corroborate what she says. My wife yesterday had in her Sunday class one of these women, naturally distinctly stupid, who for three months had, with the others, learned this system. My wife had not seen her for three or four months; she then could not read a word of her Bible, but now she held aloft one of your New Testaments, and cried, "I can read it all. I can read it all. I am so happy." You have been out here yourself, and know something of the difficulty of the Chinese characters, and so can understand what

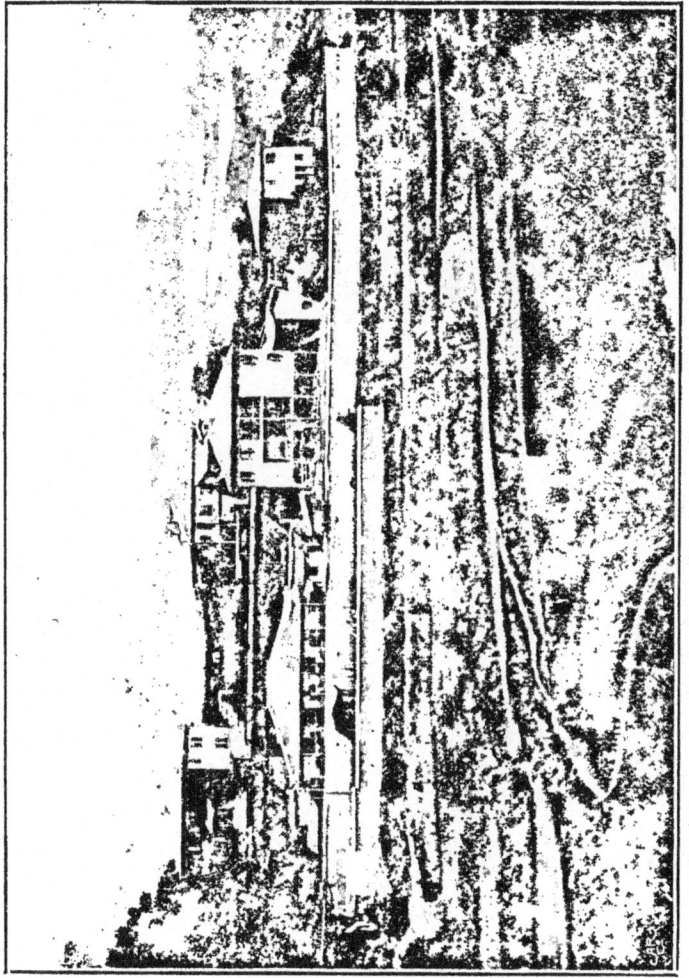

The Missionary Compound at Kucheng, containing the houses of the C.M.S. and C.E.Z.M.S.

a wonderful thing this is. I know it has cost your
Society a great deal of money, but I truly believe it is
well spent. Well, now, instead of printing more just
now in our Foochow dialect—for we have a good
quantity still in stock—I want to beg on behalf of
Kiong-ning. They are even worse off than we were,
for they have no colloquial character, and the Z.M.S.
five ladies now in the district have, in consultation
with our C.M.S. men, drawn up a system, as near as
the dialect will allow, to that adopted by us. They
(two of them) have also given the last twelve months
up to translating the New Testament into this Romanized Colloquial. This means tremendous labour, for
they had not, as we had, a character colloquial for
guide. They have spared no pains, keeping a special
Chinese teacher for the purpose, and testing his colloquial by trying it with the native women. Fortunately too, one of these ladies, Miss Bryer, is peculiarly
gifted in language, and speaks herself peculiarly well,
so that I think you may without fear accept what she
has done. The manuscript is now almost completed,
and Miss B. Newcombe, of the C.E.Z.M.S., who has just
returned Home, could give you further particulars,
and could well be trusted to revise the proof. I have
to ask you then if you will comply with their urgent
request. I trust you will say " Yes." They have had
a sale of work for the purpose, which realized something over 300 dols., and this will go to you with some
other little money given themselves. I know of
course this will go but a very short way in such an
undertaking, but it may perhaps do something to-

wards proving the reality of their belief in its being a
good work. The number of copies wanted bound at
once would not be large, for the ladies themselves must
do all the teaching. I think these numbers would be
about right: St. John's Gospel, 200 copies; four
Gospels and Acts together, fifty copies; entire New
Testaments, 100 copies, and perhaps about the same
numbers printed but not bound. Perhaps you might
think these latter numbers too small. It is hard to
prophesy what the demand will actually be; it may
catch hold of the people, and such a number as I have
given be in a couple of years exhausted. Miss B.
Newcombe's address is 12, Peafield Terrace, Black-
rock, Dublin. Thanking you again with all my heart
for what you have done for us,

Believe me, very sincerely yours,

ROBERT W. STEWART.

The Fuh-kien Province is as large as England (not
including Wales), and far more populous.

We have told of native Bible-women and catechists,
of English ladies and missionaries, of schools for children; but what are they among so many?

From Dublin a friend writes on behalf of the
friends of the Irish Church Missions, the Society in
connection with which Mrs. Stewart worked in her
youth, and received the training and teaching for
which her husband often said he felt most grateful.

The Mission workers and friends had subscribed a
considerable sum and wished to have a memorial to
Mr. and Mrs. Stewart. They proposed that the money

should be given to the Bible Society, for printing the Gospel of St. John in the Roman letters. They knew this was very near the hearts of the friends whose work they wished to help forward.

They communicated with the Society, and got for answer that they would go forward in the good work of printing the New Testament in the Kiong-ning dialect, without waiting for funds.

The Dublin Mission friends hope to send sufficient money for the Gospel of St. John. The friend who writes on behalf of the others says: "For myself I should love to think that the Gospel of St. John was being scattered on the hills where little Herbert picked his birthday flowers."

A letter comes to hand to-day where the writer says, "When I close my eyes, I can see Mr. Stewart giving his interesting descriptions, so earnestly and quietly.

"I heard him ten years ago, but I shall never forget that meeting.

"I took some notes. Here is one thing he said; 'If the Chinese held hands, they would make seven circles round the earth as great as the equator.'

"Again, 'If they began to pass a certain point two abreast, it would take seventeen and a half years for them all to pass.'"

Mr. Stewart believed in the necessity of the missionary being filled with God's Holy Spirit.

He did not lightly despise heathenism as powerless, or idol worship as a mere adoring of stocks and stones.

Through personal observation and matured thought,

M

he believed the Chinese worshipped devils, and he knew that when the strong man armed keeps his house no one but the stronger than he, the Almighty One, can cast him out.

> " It was for this that Jesus died
> On the Cross of Calvary."

"He was manifested to destroy the works of the devil."

His way of accomplishing this design is through His own people.

When the disciples asked, "Lord, wilt Thou at this time restore the kingdom to Israel?" His answer seems to me to be as if He said, "I have finished My part. The victory I have gained must be manifested through *you*—through you, when you are filled with the Spirit. *You* shall receive power."

May God raise up a band of God-possessed men and women to preach the good tidings—to live the Christ-life in China.

A standard bearer has fallen; who will take up the colours and carry them on to victory?

Robert Stewart speaks to us from the glory, "Fill up the ranks."

Louisa Stewart's life says to us, "Live Christ, and others must be blessed." The Chinese Christians from Kucheng call to us:

"Send us teachers. We have lost our spiritual father and mother."

And God says, "Whom shall We send, and who will go for Us?"

Who will say, "Here am I, send me, send me"?

CHAPTER VII

"POSSESSIONS"

CHAPTER VII

" *POSSESSIONS* " [1]

I cannot see, with my small human sight,
Why God should lead this way or that for me ;
I only know He saith, " Child, follow Me " ;—
               But I can trust.

I know not why my path should be at times
So straitly hedged, so strangely barred before ;
I only know God could keep wide the door ;—
               But I can trust.

I often wonder as, with trembling hand,
I cast the seed along the furrowed ground,
If ripened fruit for God will there be found ;—
               But I can trust.

I cannot know why suddenly the storm
Should rage so fiercely round me in its wrath ;
But this I know, God watches all my path ;—
               And I can trust.

I may not draw aside the mystic veil
That hides the unknown future from my sight ;
Nor know if for me waits the dark or light ;—
               But I can trust.

"The house of Jacob shall possess their Possessions."—OBADIAH 17.

POSSESSIONS in China ! Yes.
Let me tell you how a lady in England became heir to a whole village in China.

[1] A favourite hymn of Mrs. Stewart's in 1893, before her last journey to China.

And she is only a specimen of many others who have " interest " in that country.

There was a missionary meeting in the village where she lived—a lecture on China, illustrated by lime-light views.

Her heart was specially touched when she heard about the Bible-women. Then and there she decided to give £6 a year for one of them to be her own representative in the foreign field. She would learn her name and all she could about her work. She would pray for her and take an interest in her, and help in every way she could.

How good it is not to let the interest excited at a missionary meeting die away! Something practical should follow.

Mrs. Ahok said at a large meeting, when she saw interested faces and sympathetic tears, "I am glad you feel for my people who are without God; but that is not enough. Think before you leave your seats what you will do for China. We have a Chinese proverb—

" 'When the stove is hot
Put in the cakes.' "

A letter soon went to China carrying the good news, and an answer was received after some months from Mrs. Stewart, saying there was a young woman who had finished her training, and she could go out to teach school and visit in after hours: she was too young to travel about as the Bible-women do.

Mrs. Stewart suggested in this first letter, that our friend, instead of having a Bible-woman only, should

have a whole village of her own to care for and pray
for.

Great was her joy.

The time arrived for sending the £6 for another
year. Circumstances made it more convenient to
send £4. What could our friend do? Must she let
some one help with her village? She had so loved
to think that she had a whole village in China to
be interested in and to pray for.

Before she had come to any conclusion, she received
the following letter from Mrs. Stewart, who had
heard nothing about the matter:

KUCHENG, *January* 15, 1895.

DEAR MISS ——

Many thanks for your kind letter and enclosure
for the woman you so kindly support. The one I
have chosen for you, as I explained to my sister, is
practically the same as a Bible-woman, but we do not
call her so, for she is too young yet, according to
Chinese ideas of propriety, to travel about as much
as the regular Bible-women do. However, she is
doing quite as useful work to my mind, and we are
truly grateful for your kind help.

The £6 you send is, however, too much; £4 is all
that is needed for the women who teach, as the
travelling expenses are saved; however, if you still
like to send the £6, you will like to feel you are half
supporting another teacher!

Your woman's name I cannot remember just now,

for we generally call the women by the name of the village they come from (one of the curious customs in our part of China). Cluk-po is the name of your friend's village, and therefore she often goes by that title! I have written to one of our dear lady workers who lives at Sa-iong, the place where your woman is now working, asking her to kindly write and give you some account of her and her work, as she will know more about it than I do.

Sa-iong is a town about a day's journey from this, and for some years there seemed little hope of the people ever becoming Christians.

A chapel was opened, but so little interest was shown, that after a time, the missionary removed the catechist to a more encouraging place; and Sa-iong was left without any one to speak to the poor people of the Saviour.

Time passed on, and about eighteen months ago some of the inhabitants began to wish for some one to tell them of the true God.

They heard that in other places people were learning to worship Him, and at last a few of them came to Mr. Banister, the missionary, who preceded Mr. Stewart, asking for a teacher.

A catechist was sent; and two of our lady workers volunteered to go. They have lived there now over a year, and God is wonderfully blessing their labours.

One of them opened a day school for girls, and your woman was invited to teach them, and she has done so most faithfully. These little girls are not only learning to love the Saviour themselves, but act as little guides to the missionary ladies, leading them to visit their friends and relatives.

One of these workers tells me there are few houses now in Sa-iong where she does not find a welcome, and many have really given their hearts to God, as far as we can judge.

One remarkable instance occurred at Sa-iong last autumn of the way God honours simple faith.

There was a terrible fire in the town, and a large number of houses were burned to the ground, leaving the poor families homeless.

The people were greatly terrified, seeing the flames advancing and no means apparently of arresting their progress.

In one house, right in their path, was an old Christian woman. She climbed on the roof, and stretching her arms out towards the sky, she cried aloud to Jesus to save her.

Next day it was discovered that though the houses all round were burned, hers was untouched.

This event has much impressed even the heathen, and has led the Christians to have more simple faith in God.

One more incident I must relate about Sa-iong, for I trust it will lead you to pray even more earnestly for the poor women of China.

Miss Codrington (one of the missionary ladies) has a class of women at her own house.

She takes eight or ten at a time and teaches them for three months.

They then return to their homes. She has good hopes that nearly all she has had were really saved.

Well, one poor young thing had come from a distance. Her husband was an opium-smoker. She was staying with her father at the time she applied for admission to the school.

She was very bright and intelligent, and Miss Codrington quite loved her.

Suddenly we heard to our sorrow that her wretched husband was looking for her, and wanted to sell her!

He found her, and appeared at Sa-iong with ten men to carry her off. Miss Codrington, of course, had no power to refuse, but she made him wait till she sent for the girl's father; and very sadly she had to give her up to him.

The poor girl seemed broken-hearted, but after prayer with Miss Codrington she seemed comforted.

They spent that night in an inn, and next day some of the Christians saw the poor girl sitting in a sedan-chair, bound hand and foot with ropes.

She was taken to a village about half-a-day's journey off, and there *sold*, just as you might sell an animal! Poor young thing! Can you picture her misery?

Oh! do pray for the women and girls of China. Sad things like this occur constantly.

Women are simply bought and sold as the men please.

Yours, with grateful thanks,

LOUISA STEWART.

The £4 was given to the friend who showed the limelight views, to be sent through his "Missionary Fund."

He added £2, and so £6 was the sum again sent.

On Monday, August 5, he received the letter given below.

The same morning he read in the newspaper the telegraphic news of the translation at Hwasang.

Here is Mrs. Stewart's letter:

KUCHENG, *June* 19, 1895.

DEAR MR. BLUNDELL,

The cheque you so kindly sent for £6 has safely reached us, and we are very grateful for it. £4 from Miss —— for her native teacher, and £2 from your Missionary Fund.

You do not state what branch of the work you wish the £2 given to specially, but I presume it may also go to the schools.

We are glad to have any help just now for these schools, for we feel more and more that they are perhaps the very best means of evangelizing these great dark regions, where there is absolutely no light.

Mr. Stewart has just come back from a trip

through this large district of Kucheng, and he is quite delighted with the evident tokens of God's blessing on the schools.

He examined the children on all the leading truths of Christianity, and says they answered beautifully, better than many Sunday schools at home!

Most of these children have heathen homes, and we have heard of many instances through the year in which the parents and friends have been influenced by what the children tell them of what they learn at school.

One of our lady missionaries was invited to a house a few months ago in a village a long distance from here.

She found the idols had all been put away, and the whole family were attending the Christian services.

On asking what had led to their becoming Christians, they said that a little girl had gone to a day school in their village, and every day when she came home she repeated the hymns and verses she had learned at school.

At first they all laughed at her, but at last became interested, and finally learned to trust in the Saviour for themselves.

This is only one of many similar instances. These schools are gradually spreading the knowledge of the Saviour in a more successful way than even preaching.

Whenever my husband examines a school, the

room is packed as full as it can hold with men and boys, listening intently all the time, sometimes for two or three hours, and they learn a great deal in this way.

We are so glad to hear of the success of the lantern work, and hope that God will richly bless it. We must try and get some new slides for you.

With many thanks for all your kindness and help, and hoping you will continually remember this Province in prayer,

Believe me to be,
Yours in the Master's Service,
LOUISA STEWART.

Some people who cannot themselves go to China in the body, can go in spirit through the wonderful power of believing prayer.

Is not this the way in which Ezekiel went to that valley where the bones were " very many " and " very dry "—a very hard case?

He says, " The hand of the Lord was upon me, and He carried me out in the Spirit of the Lord, and set me down in the midst of the valley which was full of bones."

This work of intercessory prayer is not to be taken up, as our natural wishes might dictate, or our own minds decide.

" Can these bones live ? "

" O Lord, Thou knowest."

Ezekiel confesses his own ignorance.

We know not what to pray for as we ought.

" Prophesy."   " Say to them, Hear the *Word* of the Lord."

" So I prophesied as I was commanded."

The bones came together, but there was no breath.

" Come O breath, breathe upon these slain that they may live."

Ezekiel had simply said what God's Spirit spoke in him.

I am sure he did not understand.

Now God tells him, he had asked and obtained blessing upon " the whole house of Israel."

The Spirit Himself helps our infirmities and makes intercession for us.

" Whosoever shall say to this mountain be removed . . . and shall not doubt in his heart, but believes that what he saith cometh to pass, he shall have whatsoever he *saith*."

" Thou shalt decree a thing and it shall come to pass."

These promises are all made " to him that believes."

Another extract from one of Mrs. Stewart's letters cannot be omitted:

" Sometimes R. meets with such interesting characters as he goes round the station.

" One old man lately asked him to send them soon a catechist.

" ' But,' he said, ' Singang, we don't want a fine stuck-up young man, whose voice can't be heard beyond the third seat, though he may be full of wisdom inside. We want a man who goes about like the night watchman. He makes only two sounds: Pok, pok! Pok, pok!' (And the old man got up and went marching round the room imitating the way in which the watchman strikes his bamboo at night to warn the thieves). We want a man to go through the villages with a loud voice, saying, ' Jesus can save! Jesus can save!'

" Another old fellow said, when R. asked him how long he had been a Christian, 'I have known the doctrine eight years, but I have known Jesus for six years only.'

" Another, when asked how he would tell a heathen the way to heaven, said, ' I would lead him to Jesus. Jesus is the ladder to Heaven.' "

Dear Hessie Newcombe, who was bound up in the bundle of life with Robert and Louisa Stewart, gives a graphic picture of how she went campaigning, accompanied by her sister, to " take " Chinese villages for Jesus.

" For He must reign till He has put all enemies under His feet."

A Visit to a Mountain Village.

The many friends at home who have followed with prayerful interest the history of the Fuhkien Mission, must have been painfully struck with the fact, that while many of the *men* had turned from idols to God, the *women*, as a body, were almost untouched.

This state of things is the result of the peculiar

customs and habits of the Chinese, which make it an imperative necessity for women to be reached by *women.*

But now that the country has been opened up by the missionaries and catechist, there is an open field for the ladies to go in and sow seed ; yea, even to gather grain to lay at the Master's feet.

Perhaps a short account of a recent visit, which my sister and I paid to one little lonely spot, will best illustrate the truth of this statement.

It would be hard to find a place more picturesquely situated, more utterly out of the world, than the little village of Du-ling (Bamboo forest), about fourteen miles from this city (Kucheng), which we visited for the first time on November 2. The path leading to it wound round and round the mountain side ; far beneath us the river meandered in and out through the wide plain, where many of the fields were still laden with golden grain, though some had already been shorn of their beauty.

All around us we were surrounded by the luxuriant vegetation of a tropical climate. Groves of graceful bamboos, contrasting with the dark pines towering above them. Trees of every shade, from deepest crimson to the palest golden tinge, lovely clinging mosses, ferns and wild flowers, combine to form a picture of rare beauty and delight.

For utter loneliness and wildness, it reminded us most of the walk from Keswick to Wastwater, where, just as here, we seemed utterly hemmed in by the mountains.

We arrived at the village (built right on the mountain side) about 1 p.m.; and as there was no catechist living there, nor any chapel, the coolies put down our chairs just outside the village.

The first time a thing like this occurs, you do feel rather a peculiar sensation, that is, at least if you are possessed of those troublesome things called nerves. Here you are in a strange place, not knowing exactly what to do, or where to go. You cannot ask for one particular person by his surname, as probably all the inhabitants of the same locality have the same surname; and in the meantime an inquisitive crowd gathers closely round you.

However, by this time we have got accustomed to this sort of thing, and we just ask to be brought to some Christian's house.

One of the women immediately constituted herself our guide, and led us at once to the house, a room in which was used for a chapel on Sundays.

Here the women soon gathered in numbers; and after dinner, while Inie and the Bible-woman remained outside with the greater number, I took a few into our little "Prophet's Chamber," the furniture of which was as follows: a bed, consisting of boards laid on two forms, and covered with straw; a table, and one form fastened to the wall. I expect Elisha's room had the additional attraction of cleanliness, which this certainly lacked.

But these things made little impression on me at the time. That hour was one of the happiest in my life,

N

for there were seeking souls hungry for the " Bread of Life." They did not stop me to ask a single one of the usual questions as to age, family, etc.

All they knew, even the most enlightened among them, of the Christian doctrine amounted simply to this: that there was one great God, who made them and heaven and earth and all things, and who wanted them to worship Him instead of the idols, which could not help them. But, poor people, they were so eager to learn more. I can scarcely describe the awe that comes over one at such a time; you feel that God Himself is in the midst. I kept praying all the time for the right words to be given, and from the first, I think, they understood almost every word, repeating it after me.

How earnestly and attentively they listened, as by the help of the little black, red and white card, I tried to teach them something of sin, and the Saviour who came to save them, and make them holy! Just as I thought they must be getting tired, Inie knocked at the door, asking me to come out and play the concertina, saying that in the outer room the women had been just as eager to listen. I played and sang " Jesus loves me " over and over again, and they soon joined in. Then Inie asked them a few simple questions, and their ready answers showed how the previous lessons had been taken in and understood. That evening four or five of them learnt Miss Marsh's prayer printed on the back of Mrs. Grimke's cards.

Next morning (Saturday), as our house was up above the village, we went down to one of the houses below. Here the women gathered in such numbers that we had no opportunity for individual talking. The noise was sometimes almost deafening, but the concertina generally created a lull. It is sometimes hard to remember that it is from such sowing times are gathered the few earnest ones, who afterwards come one by one to learn more.

One thing which greatly pleased us was the readiness with which those who knew a little themselves tried to teach others.

In the afternoon some of the women came again, asking us to teach them, and it certainly is true that God does open their understanding. They asked me to teach them the Creed, and I was perfectly amazed how they took in its meaning. Even when we came to the "Communion of Saints," they seemed to see at once that as Christians we became as sisters, having the one great Father and the one Saviour to talk to each other about.

That evening we had a prayer-meeting in Martha's house, as I surnamed her. She certainly was a character! A middle-aged woman, with a fat, good-humoured face, possessed of ceaseless energy, both of hands and tongue. The former she fortunately used in the unusual business of keeping her house clean, as well as in dragging women by main force to listen, and then preparing all kinds of dainties, which she heaped upon both willing and unwilling guests. Her words poured forth like torrents. We always felt thankful if we could just catch the drift of the long oration. Yet she was so eager to learn, and to get others to learn: we felt she was, indeed, a friend, and yet one of those who give you a slightly uneasy feeling, as you are not quite sure what extraordinary thing she may do next.

But this village has also its Mary. How we were drawn together those few days! A quiet, grave young woman, so gentle and earnest, who seemed to drink in every word, and think it all over in her own mind. I expect much from her influence in the future.

On Sunday a great many came over from the adjoining village, where, as yet, there are neither Christians nor enquirers. But we are praying that the light which cannot be hid may soon spread to them also. One woman listened very attentively, and said she would come again. We visited the village in the afternoon. At first it seemed useless to try and talk to such a crowd as had assembled, but Inie at last gained the attention of a few. She noticed the fixed gaze of one young opium-smoker in the background, and it was very interesting to find the same young man coming and spending the whole of the next morning with one of the Christians.

On Monday afternoon I went down with the Bible-woman to Martha's house. At this time of the year the women are very busy drying and sunning their rice, so that it is hard to get them together, but Mary and one or two others came up. Martha did not at first appear, and I soon found to my cost that she was on hospitality intent, as in about half an hour she appeared, triumphantly carrying some soft, red cakes, that looked like soap, but were really made of rice cooked in oil. Out of common politeness, of course, I had to eat a little.

That hour I did enjoy so much. The Bible-woman read and expounded from our little catechism on the "Life of our Lord," and I found out the references in the Bible, Mary reading them after me. When we came to the history of our Lord's sufferings I read it straight from the Bible. Never before had it all seemed so real to myself as then, when I saw how *they* felt it. Mary shuddered all over when it came to the crown of thorns, the spitting and the scourging, and she said over and over again, "And He suffered it all *willingly* for us! Truly we should love Him and try to please Him."

When I asked her would she not try and tell others the good news, she said so earnestly that indeed she would.

Now, dear friends, why have I written all this? First of all, because I do want you so much to pray earnestly, perseveringly, believingly, for these young Du-ling Christians.

You can have no idea of the awful temptations and difficulties by which they are surrounded. Satan's power is tremendous in this land, but our God is strong to deliver. Oh, do pray for them. "Satan to Jesus must bow."

Then I do want you to pray that the eagerness to learn may soon be the rule, not, as now, the exception. This is the Holy Spirit's work.

"Pray louder, pray longer, for the great gift of fire
    To come down on these hearts with its whirlwinds of grace."

The Master came to seek and to save the lost. Dear sisters, ask yourselves, are you, as He was, seeking the lost? Surely if any are the lost ones it is these poor women, led captive by Satan at his will.

Oh! for hearts laid low at the Master's feet! Oh, for burnt lips which will only cry, "Lord, what wilt Thou have me to do!" Then soon, very soon, our King, Jesus, would reign triumphantly in this land.

HESSIE NEWCOMBE.

In a later letter Miss Newcombe writes:—

". . . The time at Du-ling was most remarkable. I think there is quite a revival there. One felt so completely in the hands of the Spirit, so utterly taken out of oneself, only a mere instrument. . . ."

The following extracts from the journals of Miss Newcombe and Miss Clara Bradshaw (now Mrs. E. C. Millard) give interesting descriptions of travelling in China, and bring before our minds in a forcible manner the great need of workers in this vineyard of the Lord:—

"We left Foochow early on Tuesday morning, and in about four hours we reached Kuang-tau, and climbing over the side of the launch, found ourselves in a sanpan which took us to shore. Our cook hired native chairs for us, made as light as possible for mountain climbing, with bamboo seats and poles, and a covering of matting.

" We only stopped once on the road to Leing-kong city, and arrived there towards evening. It is a lovely place, and from the little room we slept in we could get on to the roof outside, looking over the river and long bridge made of such huge pieces of granite stone, some little houses stuck up on the end of it, and grand ranges of mountains with such jagged edges on the opposite side.

" We rested for a while, and then thought we would go out and look about. We found ourselves in a street, and stopping to ask some women had they ' eaten their rice yet?' conversation commenced; we soon had quite a crowd, and I believe some were really listening, and trying to take in what seems so hard for them to understand, how Jesus loves them, and wants to save them.

" We came in and enjoyed our meal of fish and rice, and being tired, thought of going to bed, when the door opened, and in came a number of women to be talked to. They remained till quite late, but we were very glad of the opportunity, and hope to stay some nights there when on our way back to Foochow.

"Next morning on we went, through most lovely scenery, and in the evening reached Lo-nguong.

" Next day and the day following were very wet, such rain as I think I never saw at home. We had time for rest, and waiting on Him to renew our strength and give us wisdom in all things.

" As I was writing, in came a message to say some one had come to lead us to a house where they wanted to hear ' the Doctrine.' So we went, and there stayed till the evening with *such* crowds; they listened wonderfully well, and five or six women seemed to take in the message.

"On Saturday morning the weather cleared a little, and we went to a village where there are some Christian women; we had our midday meal in one of their houses, and such a feast was prepared for us! But we could not satisfy them, however much we swallowed. They having fed our bodies, it was time for us to feed their souls, and yet it scarcely seemed like ' feeding' their souls, for oh! the black darkness of those minds! Poor people! I do think if you in England could only realize the need of workers, surely more would come.

"I remember at home parishioners were not satisfied if a clergyman's visit was not paid at each *house* at least once a year; I wonder how they would like instead to have the *city* of Dublin only receive one visit in the year? So it is with many of the places here, where there are a few Christians; the Missionary can only pay one visit to the place and have a general meeting, sometimes not as often as once a year. And then think of the numbers of heathen cities and villages that as yet have *never* been visited.

"From the little window of our room here we see a very high hill; a long steep path of stone steps goes right over the mountain, and since we arrived I have not seen the long line of people passing up and down those steps cease. It seems an endless stream of immortal souls. Nearly all of them are burden-bearers carrying loads, and as I see them I think of the way

their bodies and souls are weighed down, the slaves of
Satan; my heart goes out in prayer for them, and I
plead with the King to send forth—no, '*thrust forth*'
—some of His soldiers to free those slaves of Satan
fast bound in misery and iron. They pass before our
eyes, and we know we shall never see them again
until they pass by the Great White Throne. Can you
imagine how we pray for them?

"Sunday was another pouring wet day. That night
we had special prayer to know how to get better at the
people, and I think the prayer was speedily answered.
Next day we went out visiting quite early in the
morning, but could not move beyond one house, for
there we had such numbers to speak to. It is difficult
to know what to do with the *men*, for if they come the
women won't, so in this house we had them all turned
out. In a few minutes I looked up and saw the same
congregation of men assembled on the top of the *roof*
of the next house, looking right in on us.

"One dear old woman with white hair seemed greatly
impressed, but Satan was as busy as ever, and when
we pressed her to leave her idols and come to God, she
vanished in a second out of the room. Satan so often
seems to do that; sometimes the whole crowd of
listeners suddenly jump up, and in a moment disappear,
and one cannot get them back again.

"We returned to the city for our midday meal, and
then started again to a house at some distance, where
they 'received us gladly.' Here I counted fifty
women listening, and the large doorway was quite

crowded up by men, so that soon we wondered where we should get air to breathe, much less room to move. A woman and a girl beside me were so interested, and asked me to repeat anything they did not understand.

"Next day we started early for a village a good way off, and walked there. Such numbers of villages we passed by, where the people all came out to look at us! How we longed to stop at all these places, but we knew we must not; at some we promised to go another time. At last we reached the village we were seeking; there we found a Christian woman, and in her tiny hut sat down on stools; very soon this little house was quite too full, and we had to disperse the crowd, which not only filled the house, but the narrow street outside, by promising them we would meet them in a larger place (the Bible-woman explaining to them where), and tell them the 'Doctrine.' As we were doing this tea was brought, and also eggs and chopsticks, which we ate, and then continued talking. But I don't feel I can give you any idea of the crowd, or how they pressed on us, not to mention pigs, etc. We went on as long as we could, and then had to push our way through for fresh air.

"We spent the night in the house of a Christian widow—such a nice bright little woman. She had been the wife of a catechist, and could read St. Matthew and St. Mark, so every morning and evening she holds prayers in her house for the villagers, a most remarkable thing for a *woman* in China to do, but as she could only read these two Gospels, the people never heard any of the rest of the Bible."

From Lo-nguong city Miss Newcombe and Miss Bradshaw, accompanied by Seng-lai, the wife of the Chinese clergyman, made a tour round the Mission Stations to the west of the city, which they thus describe :—

"*Monday.*—Started from Lo-nguong early, in chairs. Got along slowly ; roads bad after rain. Went nine miles by eleven o'clock, which brought us to the village of Heng-long. While the people of the house were cooking rice for us, we had a splendid opportunity of delivering our message. First we invited the women into our little bedroom, but it was soon filled to suffocation, and there were more coming, so the catechist suggested the little chapel, which was airy and large, and opened on to the street. We went in, and in two minutes it was packed. There must have been considerably over 100 people, men and women, in it. We got on the raised platform, and had a good talk with them about John iii. 16, finding out by questions that some were following what was said.

"After dinner we started for O-iong in pours of rain. It was nine miles all uphill, and at times so steep that we got out and walked, to ease the burden for the poor coolies. We reached our destination a little after four o'clock, the rain still pouring, in spite of which the little upstairs room we were shown into soon was densely packed with women.

"Only one European lady had ever passed through this part of the country before, so our arrival everywhere created intense excitement. We could do but little talking, as we were so tired, and the people so packed, that they were continually getting on the top of each other, or, worse still, on the top of some poor little three or four-year-old, too small to be seen, this causing a serious commotion.   We tried singing ' Jesus loves me ' to quiet them down, and were rather surprised at its effect ; they were evidently frightened, for they made a rush for the door, tumbling over each other in their hurry to get out, and we had some difficulty in persuading them that there was nothing to fear.

" *Tuesday.*—Before we were up this morning, from sounds going on downstairs we knew people were waiting to see us, and it was with great difficulty we kept our room free from visitors till our dressing was finished.   Breakfast over, we came out into the hall, and did our best to speak to the people.   I never saw such a sight, a great mass of people swaying backwards and forwards.   We tried again and again to get a hearing, but it seemed hopeless, so we made for a door at the back of the hall, and, standing there, let none but women pass; in they filed, till every inch was filled, and they were standing out in the yard beyond. We had a really good time, some women listening most attentively as we went through the ' Wordless Book,' and showing by their answers they had taken in what we were saying.   By twelve o'clock we were nearly exhausted, and fortunately the women wanted to go home to dinner, so we escaped by a back way, and got to our room unnoticed, barred the door, and had a good rest.

"We had determined after dinner to have first a quiet time with the Christian women before meeting the crowds again. They lived at some distance, and it was a pouring wet day, which accounted for the fact that, while we had crowds of heathen from the village, we had not seen the Christians before. There were seven or eight baptized women, and one woman and her daughter wishing for baptism. We began by asking them each how long they had been Christians, what they had worshipped before; and then, which was best, the idols, or God ; and why God was best.

"They did not seem to understand this way of putting the question, so we asked, 'All the years you worshipped idols, what did you get from them?' They confessed, 'Nothing at all.' 'And all the years you have worshipped God, what have you had from Him?' We got some nice answers ; one woman said, she day by day received the Holy Spirit's help, both for what she did, and for what she said. Another said, the Holy Spirit daily helped her to do right. A third said, she had obtained forgiveness. We then had a little talk about prayer, and tried to encourage those who were still but beginning to worship to pray in their own words to God, words they themselves understood, for what they really wanted. We closed with a prayer-meeting, in which *all* joined, prayers short and to the point, and we felt thankful for this evidence that the message had been received. Some had evidently prayed aloud for the first time.

"Our little meeting over, we arranged with the

catechist's wife, who had been at the Foochow Women's School for nearly two years, to have a special meeting for the women, before the ordinary Church Service on Sunday. After a short rest, we had to go down once more, to find another crowd of men and women waiting for us. But this time we had a really good opportunity. The Spirit was evidently present in power, compelling them to listen, and convincing them. Several were solemnized, who at first had lightly said that they knew the 'Doctrine,' and had heard it all before. At last, when we went upstairs, after a few closing words entreating them not to despise God's message, there was evidently a prolonged conversation with the catechist before some of them returned home.

" *Wednesday.*—Early after breakfast we started for Cai-tau, a village three miles off, where we heard there were six or seven Christian women. On getting there, however, we found not one of them had been baptized, or indeed knew anything about God or Christ at all. It was very sad; they called themselves Christians, and were so, just in so far as they did not worship idols, but no further. We asked the reason, and were told, that being three or four miles from the nearest Church, they could not possibly, on their bound feet, walk there over that rough hilly road; and we felt this was true, as with our large feet and good sound boots, we had felt quite tired out, after walking over that morning.

" One of these women is a catechist's wife. We

spoke to him and asked him how it was. He said, 'She is a *woman*; women are too stupid and dull to take in anything!' You may feel inclined to blame *him*, but I feel inclined to blame *ourselves*, their Christian sisters at home and abroad, who have done so little towards bringing them that Gospel of Salvation, which we ourselves prize so dearly!

"That night was spent at Ching-kang, and the next morning in talking with heathen women, who came *en masse.*' They had 'never before seen a foreign lady, or heard the Doctrine.'

"*Thursday.*—Iong-tau. We had a very hot time in the sun. The path was one long ascent; I don't think I had ever been up such a perpendicularly steep ascent. We arrived about two o'clock feeling very tired and very hot. . . . It is now evening; we have had the people pressing round us the whole afternoon, and now I am afraid I sympathize with the disciples, when they asked for the multitudes to be sent away.

"*Friday.*—Lau-iong. Last night we had the most tremendous thunderstorm I ever heard. The lightning followed, flash after flash in quick succession, and the peals of thunder, rolling and roaring on the top of each other incessantly, sounded exactly as if great rocks were being smashed in pieces. Then the rain commenced, and went on getting heavier and heavier. I could not have imagined rain falling could have made such a noise.

"After breakfast we started in chairs, which we were

thankful to obtain, for we were tired. We had thought yesterday that we had gone as high as roads could carry us, but we still found ourselves going up step by step, till at last valleys and depths were quite lost to sight, and nothing was to be seen around us but a wavy billowy sea of mountain tops. It was bitterly cold, and the rain poured, but we reached this in good time, and have had a really delightful time downstairs, the people listening splendidly ; and though the room was full, and a large crowd of men were standing at the door, there was perfect quiet, while we told the Story of the Cross from the ' Wordless Book.' We were *so* very thankful for the women who had never heard before. At first they seemed unable to take in anything, but before we left some had certainly got hold of the main points. Oh! when will our English sisters take compassion on these lost sheep, and come to seek and save them ? "

Saturday and Sunday were spent at A-chia, where there was not much to encourage, and on Monday they travelled through magnificent scenery to Uongpuang, which was reached about midday. They write :—

" The crowds here were gathered to meet us, and we are in a nice clean little loft, outside the house, with a ladder to get up to it. We had a little gathering of Christians this afternoon. It was very fine. They told us how they had become Christians, and what two said struck me very much. They had heard of our God, but had not believed, until one had got very ill, and prayed our God to make her well, which He did, and both women believed on Him, and have worshipped Him ever since. Afterwards we went to the heathen, and tried to tell them the way of salvation.

"We left Uong-puang early next morning as soon as our last entreaties to the people to believe in Jesus were ended, and reached Sioh-piek about noon."

A day, fully occupied up to twelve o'clock at night, was spent at Sioh-piek, and the following day the ladies returned to their starting point, the city of Longuong. They write:—

"We came back here with hearts overflowing to God, with thanks for all His mercies and goodness to us, in this our first tour in this district. How wonderfully He has kept us, and has, I believe, given us confidence and faith, to expect the 'greater things,' throughout this whole vast Province.

"On coming back here, the first news we heard at the gate was, that in one of the houses we had been visiting, the old woman with whom we had pleaded so especially, but who had run away when pressed to decide, had passed into eternity. Oh! time *is* short, soon the chance of writing home and asking you to come and help, in prayer and every way you can, will be over. The fields here *are* truly white unto harvest, the labourers *are* few. 'Pray ye,' 'Come ye,' and share with us in the glory of the Harvest Home.

"For your Father's sake, who loves these lost ones, for Jesus' sake, who died for them, be up and doing. *Come*; souls are dying without having heard of life. Is it *your* fault? Why are you not out among the

o

heathen, telling them the good news that has flooded
your own soul with light and joy ?

"When I hear, as I do in letters from the Homeland,
of Gospel meetings, at one of which there are three or
four Christian workers if it is a small meeting, and
far more if a large one, I do feel jealous.   Did Christ
not die for China ?   Are these Chinese sisters less dear
to Christ than our English or Irish ones, that for
one who will go to the heathen, there are hundreds to
speak to the people at home?   If you but offer to the
Lord that which costs you nothing, think you He will
accept it at your hand ?   Your staying at home is
withholding blessing, alike on the work you cling to
so closely, as well as on the neglected field you are
leaving untilled.

"God is with us for our Captain.   'Come ye to the
help of the Lord against the mighty.'"

On their return to headquarters they write :—

"Back again in civilization, knives, forks, spoons,
etc., and wishing to be out of it, and back again to
the chopsticks of these last happy weeks.

"Our first visit to Lo-nguong is over, and with it
our first attempt for any lengthened period to live on
native food, and we have seldom felt in better health.
We mention this, as it seems God's seal of approval
on this effort to bridge over the chasm between us
and the people.   Anything that brings us nearer to
them, and makes us more like one of themselves, is
well worth doing for Jesus' sake, who, when He came
to save us, became of one bone and flesh with us,
and was 'not ashamed to call us brethren.'"

CHAPTER VIII

HANDS CLASPED

"I the Lord thy God will hold thy right hand, saying unto thee, Fear not ; I will help thee."—ISAIAH xli. 13.

CHAPTER VIII

HANDS CLASPED

Hold Thou my hand! so weak I am and helpless,
   I dare not take one step without Thy aid ;
Hold Thou my hand! for then, O loving Saviour,
   No dread of ill shall make my soul afraid.

Hold Thou my hand! and closer, closer draw me
   To Thy dear self—my hope, my joy, my all ;
Hold Thou my hand, lest haply I should wander ;
   And, missing Thee, my trembling feet should fall.

Hold Thou my hand! the way is dark before me
   Without the sunlight of Thy face divine ;
But when by faith I catch its radiant glory,
   What heights of joy, what rapturous songs are mine !

Hold Thou my hand! that when I reach the margin
   Of that lone river Thou didst cross for me,
A heavenly light may flash along its waters,
   And every wave like crystal bright shall be.

IT seemed touching to receive letters from them in
September, written in July when they were so
peacefully resting in their mountain retreat from the
heat of the plains.

Mr. and Mrs. Stewart, with five children, and Lena,
the nurse (whose history forms the last chapter of
this book); Miss Nellie and Miss Maud Saunders

(called Topsy for a pet name) staying with them, occupying what last year was the nursery, a new nursery having been added to the cottage this year, " made of clay which had hardened in the sun."

These dear girls, Nellie and Topsy Saunders, were quite young, not much over twenty years of age either of them.

Mr. Eugene Stock writes in the *Gleaner* of September, 1895 :—

" Of my dear young friends, Harriette Elinor Saunders (Nellie), and Elizabeth Maud Saunders (Topsy), I must speak personally. They were the firstfruits of our Australian visit.

" They had given themselves wholly to the Lord for His service during Mr. George Grubb's mission some months before, and on the very evening of our landing, Sunday, April 24, 1892, they responded to Mr. Stewart's first sermon by an enquiry about going to China. They were the two children of a widowed mother, and the plan was that all three should go together. . . . They proposed to go as honorary missionaries. . . . Financial failures took away almost all their property, and when the Victoria Association (of the C.M.S.) proposed to send all three out upon its funds, the dear mother said her girls should go, but she would stop until she could realize what was left, and then follow at her own charges.

" But the two years that have since elapsed have not brought the necessary means to her; and now— ! "

Some weeks passed by, and in a private letter Mr. Stock again mentions Mrs. Saunders.

"I have heard from Australia. All Melbourne went into mourning; services were held in the churches. Mrs. Saunders is triumphant."

If she did not "realize" the money she expected, she realized in the hour of need what strong consolation God is to them who put their trust in Him.

When we read the words, "Mrs. Saunders is triumphant," how we praise God—her God and our God!

There is no separation to those who dwell in God; and so we in this hemisphere clasped her hand in that hemisphere; and though the natural mother's heart in Nellie and Topsy Saunders' mother, and in Louisa Stewart's mother, must have been pierced, yet together their voices ascended in praise to Him who doeth all things well.

No murmuring spoiled the melody, no useless regrets dimmed the glory of the martyr's crown.

Annie Gordon too was among the firstfruits of Australia unto God, willingly obeying the call to a missionary's life.

Elsie Marshall and Lucy Stewart had gone from happy English homes; both, I think, had heard the call to China through Mr. Stewart's preaching.

Last, but not least, of this "noble army of martyrs," comes dear Hessie Newcombe.

She and her elder sister were the pioneer missionaries in this woman's work for women in China.

Slight and delicate-looking, she endured hardship as a good servant of Jesus Christ. She really "took pleasure" in what, naturally speaking, would have been great trials.

Many entries in her journal show how lightly she esteemed her own discomfort.

When travelling with a native Bible-woman, herself in Chinese dress, sleeping sometimes in a temple, sometimes in an inn, one night she did not get continuous sleep. The rats running over her face woke her up, but she soon went to sleep again.

Robert Stewart has more than once said of her and her sister missionaries:

"You could not find more devoted and successful missionaries, I feel sure, anywhere." And he was not a man who spoke carelessly or at random. He meant what he said.

Words are poor and cold, when we try to tell of such lives, truly lived in the secret place of the Most High.

From personal acquaintanceship with dear Hessie I can say, she lived the Christ-life. He lived in her, He filled her being, He looked through her eyes, He spoke in and through her. Not only in China has she been used of God, but in her own native Ireland many rise up and call her blessed. In England her life and words have left a sweet savour of Christ wherever she has been.

Mrs. Stewart's letters tell of the two houses, and how Nellie and Topsy Saunders were under their own roof, and next door those already mentioned, with Miss Codrington (the "Flora" of Miss Tolley's journal), the Elisha who remains to us (together with Mr. Stewart's three children) to carry on the work in the spirit of Elijah, or rather to show that the "Lord God of Elijah" is still on earth,—that He still dwells with "him who is of a contrite and humble spirit."

Rev. W. H. S. Phillips, a brother missionary and a brother beloved in the Lord, "sleeping in a house five minutes walk off, though spending most of the day with the Stewarts" (I quote from his own letter), also left behind, completes the list of this happy family of missionaries. The mountains round Ku-cheng having become literally to some of them "the land of Beulah."

Mr. Stewart, writing to one of his relations not long before his last leave-taking, said: "It seems like a kind of dying, this going away; but He holds our hands, and the hands of the loved ones we leave behind, and so it is all well.

"'God holds the key of all unknown, and I am glad :
If other hands should hold the key, or if He trusted it to me,
I might be sad.'"

"He holds our hands" is an allusion to the hymn at the beginning of this chapter, a great favourite with him.

He sang it with his children every morning at prayers that last summer he had them all round him for a bright, brief holiday in North Wales.

But let no one think he went sadly. No, he (and she too) "loved" to be with the children, when that was "His sweet will"; and equally loved to go to China when His voice called them; the secret being this: they loved God, and knew He loved them, with a real, tender, sympathizing love; and so they knew His will could be nothing but good to them, their children, and every one concerned.

> "Ill that He blesses is our good,
>   And unblest good is ill :
> And all is right that seems most wrong,
>   If it be His sweet will."

I believe both Robert and Louisa Stewart had passed through real death—death to the self-life.

When God through the Spirit spoke those words in their inmost hearts, "Ye are dead," they believed God, and they passed through the experience described in Hebrews iv. 12, the dividing of soul and spirit—a very real death.

I remember how she spoke to me about this subject when I stayed with her in Bedford—too sacred to repeat even now.

"A sword shall pass through thine own soul also."

"My soul is even as a weaned child." "*Knowing* this, that our old man (self) was crucified with Him." These, and other precious words given by God, were passed on by her to me. She said she found trials were so different now to what they had been, because now there was no rebellion, no questioning. She had learned to count it all joy, when she fell into divers trials.

I remember how she said, her face all aglow, as it always was when she spoke of China, "I do not quite understand, but I believe our death means life to the Chinese."

I said, "Is not that what the Apostle Paul meant when he said, 'death worketh in us and life in you?'"

She said, with her accustomed humility, "I will ask God to teach me."

We knelt and prayed, asking for that teaching, or rather that Teacher, who is never asked for in vain. I remembered afterwards that she had pleaded this verse in prayer, asking that death in them bringing life to the Chinese might be made by God a practical experience in herself and her husband. He was then in Australia on a missionary tour with Mr. Stock.

After his return I was at Bedford again. One of the first things he said to me was, that while he was far away that verse had come to him with great power and new light; and he remarked, "It makes one love the thought of death, now that we know it means life to the Chinese."

Yes: "If it die," said the Master, "it bringeth forth much fruit."

Words spoken first of Himself, and then of every one of His true followers. True to-day. This "fruit," though possibly found "after many days," is certain; it cannot fail.

He passed through the experience first, He asks us to follow.

He knew that if we would wear the crown, we must take up the cross (death to the self-life) and follow Him.

" And " (rich reward) " where I am there shall also My servant be."

" Whosoever liveth and believeth in Me shall never die. Believest thou this ? "

" Yea, Lord," we answer. And so we know our loved ones did not see death. They entered into the life that is life indeed.

William Dell, preaching before Oliver Cromwell, said :—

" This crucified flesh only is able to endure the will of God and to suffer for His Name. For till the flesh be crucified with Christ, and killed by the Word, it will suffer nothing for God, but will by all possible means avoid the cross; but when it is truly crucified, it will endure the greatest evils that can be inflicted on it, either by men or devils, or by the Lord Himself, and that with much willingness and cheerfulness. . . . And as this crucified flesh will suffer anything for God, so it will suffer it aright . . . first, in obedience to God; . . . secondly, in meekness and patience as Christ; . . . and thirdly, in love, and that to the very persecutors, so as to pity them and pray for them. This is a glorious suffering indeed, and no flesh can suffer thus but this crucified flesh . . . As it is able to suffer all things, so also it is able to overcome all things . . . It is quickened with Christ to overcome all things. . . .

" That flesh which is crucified by the Word and the Spirit is thereby made superior to all things in that exaltation and might which the Word and Spirit communicate to it."

The following letters from Louisa Stewart, dated July 6 and July 19, 1895, both written from Hwasang, and received by us at Peel, the first on August 30, the second on September 6,—spoke to us of trust and peace and earthly quiet. They seemed to say to us too, " We are happier now than you can picture ; the veil of the flesh has been manifestly rent, from top to bottom. Do you wish us back again ? "

The description in the first of these letters of the walk up the hill, in the night, was used by God greatly to comfort Mrs. Stewart's mother.

At night, before she slept, yet not fully awake, came the words with heavenly sweetness, " *He* set His face as a flint to go to Jerusalem." And these thoughts came unbidden. " This was repeated in that walk to Hwasang. It was the Christ Himself who once more set His face as a flint to 'go up' to the place of suffering. He knew, though they did not, what lay before them. And knowing it all, He upheld them by the right hand of His righteousness, He held their right hands, as He had promised, and He guided them. He carried them to the cottage home at Hwasang.

" Once more He rejoiced in His Father's will, even

though it meant suffering to His precious children, even as He had said, ' Not My will, but Thine be done,' when it meant for Him the cross and the grave."

One, to whom she told of the comfort " wherewith she had been comforted of God," gave her a copy of the following beautiful lines by Christina Rossetti:—

" Up Thy hill of sorrows,
    Thou, all alone,
Jesus, man's Redeemer,
    Climbing to a throne.
Through the world triumphant,
    Through the Church in pain,
Who think to look upon Thee
    No more again.

Upon my hill of sorrows,
    I, Lord, with Thee,
Cheered, upheld, yea carried,
    If a need should be.
Cheered, upheld, yea, carried,
    Never left alone,
Carried in Thy heart of hearts
    To a throne."

Extract from Mrs. Stewart's letter, received by us August 30 :—

"Hwasang, *July* 6.

"You will see by the heading of my letter that we are again established in our summer quarters. The children and Lena went up about a fortnight before we did, as the heat was very great at Kucheng, and we could not leave till the work closed for the summer.

"Monday, Topsy Saunders came from her country

station. Tuesday we packed up, and in the afternoon she and I went to pay Dr. Gregory a visit. . . .

"Next day, Wednesday, we got up early to send off our loads before the sun got very hot, and we arranged that our chair-coolies should come for us after dinner, as we should then reach the mountains in the cool of the day. We had our dinner, and then the cook with the few remaining things started off, and we patiently waited for the coolies. No one appeared. We sent a man to inquire. The answer came back that they could not go that day, but would arrive at 'day dawn.' What was to be done? . . . We held a council of war, and decided to walk all the way, twelve miles. We could not start till the day began to cool, but as there was a moon it did not matter. The first part of our walk was very flat, and led along by the bed of the river, and just as it was getting dusk, we reached the foot of the mountain. . . . The moon soon rose, and we had quite light enough to see our way, and it was so beautifully cool and the mountain air so fresh we did not get very tired. The last piece is a very steep pull, and we sat down to rest before attempting it. We were met there by a man with a lantern, who had come from the house to meet us. We got in about ten o'clock and found the little girls still up watching for us. Hessie Newcombe and Lucy Stewart were also looking out for us, so we had a good welcome. . . .

"It has been rather wet since we came up, so we have not been able to go out much, but it is *such* a change from Kucheng; we can actually have a blanket on at night and enjoy it! We had a new room built on to the house this year, which is a great improvement. It makes a fine big nursery, and the former little nursery we have given to Nellie and Topsy Saunders, so we have a large family!

"In the Z.M.S. house next door we have Hessie Newcombe, Flora Codrington, Lucy Stewart; and two others are coming shortly, Elsie Marshall and Annie Gordon. We hope to have some good times together, specially during Keswick week." (Then come many interesting little details, stories of the children, etc.)

"This letter seems all family news: holiday time is not so good for writing about work. But one joyful thing I must tell you—Flora Codrington was able to carry on her Station Class, though we had to close ours when we went to Foochow, and as an experiment she taught four women to read in Roman character. She had them just three months and a fortnight, and when the time came for them to go all four could read quite well and find all their places in the New Testament quite quickly. We hope great things from these Station Classes now we find the women can learn in three months. We hope to have *your* house [1] full again early in September, so please to remember to pray for the women."

[1] This refers to the house built at Kucheng for native Bible-women by many friends at home, who sent their gifts through Mrs. Smyly.

EXTRACTS FROM MRS. STEWART'S LAST LETTER,
RECEIVED SEPT. 6.

"Hwasang, *July* 19.

"Your letter last mail told us that you had just
heard of our flight into the city for fear of the
Vegetarians. God is indeed good in keeping you free
from anxiety. We had special prayer in the boat
going down to Foochow, that God would keep all the
dear ones at home 'in perfect peace,' and He did
answer certainly.

"It was a most strange affair altogether, but it was
really the Japanese coming south and threatening to
bombard Foochow that gave the Vegetarians courage
to threaten an attack on Kucheng. They are really
rebels against their own Government, but they have
small chance of doing any mischief except in times of
trouble from an outside foe. The present Government
is so hated by the people that there would certainly be
a rebellion if there seemed any hope of success. God
has wonderfully answered prayer, however, and restored peace, and already we see signs that God is
going to bring good out of all the evil. In many
places there is a greater spirit of enquiry than ever
before, and some of the Christians say they have
learned to *trust* in prayer as never before.

"We are feeling much the better for our change to
this cool place—not one ill. Is not that cause for great
thankfulness to God? . . It is such a pretty place
too. We spend our days very quietly; we have to stay
indoors till 5 o'clock, and we spend the time at lessons,

P

reading aloud, writing letters, and looking after the children. From 5 o'clock to 7 o'clock all who are inclined go for a walk, and the sisters from the other house join us. Some days they go to the village and talk to the women, and twice a week come here for prayer and Bible-reading. Sunday Robert and I go to the village and have a sort of informal service for the heathen. Sometimes a good many come, sometimes only a few, but we find by experience that more come when there are not too many of us 'foreigners' together. One old man seemed really interested. He has come several times, and last Sunday he turned to the rest of the congregation and said, ' Truly the words are good. They say our sins can be forgiven, and that the Saviour died for us, and will allow us to go to His home in Heaven.' He gave them a second edition of what we had been saying. We were very glad, for it showed us he had taken it all in himself.

"Linda Wade is spending the holidays at Kuliang, also Annie Tolley, Fanny Burroughs, and Maude Newcombe. The house here can only take in six, so they take it in turn to go to Kuliang.

.   .   .   .   .

" The two little boys are very well just now. Herbert is growing much stronger than he was; just at this moment they are together in a swing we had put up in the verandah. Evan sits in the middle of the seat and Herbert stands with one foot on each side of him, and works the swing up ever so high. They scream so loudly with delight that Lena has to rush

out to hush them every now and then, to let baby
sleep. Baby is looking better, and is growing very
amusing."

.   .   .   .   .

Her last description of her Chinese life, quiet and
happy, her ears filled with the laughter of her little
boys, her heart full of love and longing for the
heathen, and of care for the dear missionary sisters
and for her own family !

The week after was their " Keswick week," given
up more especially to praise and prayer, study of
God's Word and exhorting one another.

Mr. Phillips' letter, written after all was over, tells
a little of this quiet week, their " retreat " among the
hills :

" It seemed as if God were specially preparing all
for His own presence.

" The week before had been a specially helpful time,
our ' Keswick week.' Every one seemed to get something from the Master Himself for mutual food.

" Dear Mr. Stewart was very full, and dear Mrs.
Stewart gave us a wonderful Bible - reading on 2
Chronicles xx.

" She was such a mother in the Mission ; all who
knew her thanked God for knowing her. I never
heard a native say a word except of love and rever-
ence for her.

" On the day before the riot (Wednesday) we had a
Bible-reading on the Transfiguration, little thinking
that the immediate glory was so near for some.

"On the Thursday we were to have had a picnic to keep Herbie's birthday, and the poor little fellow could not sleep on Wednesday night for excitement."

On Thursday morning early another letter tells us little Herbert went out with his sisters to gather flowers, and then came the end—no, not the end, the sudden entrance into glory, the beginning of life.

The assassins took the sheets from the beds to make banners. On one they wrote:—

"The Dragon will conquer the foreigners' GOD."

"'The Son of God goes forth to war' also, and we *know* He is Victor. To Him every knee shall bow, every tongue confess that He is Lord. Poor, blinded Vegetarians, followers, as they themselves confess, of the Dragon, fighting under his banner! 'The Dragon fought and his angels, and prevailed not, neither was their presence found any more in heaven.'

"Stephen prayed for his murderers, a maddened crowd who stoned him, and for Saul, who was consenting unto his death.

"God answered that prayer in the case of Saul becoming the Apostle Paul.

"May there not be a Paul among these blinded, deluded, we believe devil-possessed men? These devils can come forth by nothing but prayer. Oh! that God's Holy Spirit may cause such a mighty, united prayer to go up to God for China, for the heathen, for these special haters of the 'foreigners' God,' that many may become obedient to the faith. With God all things are possible."

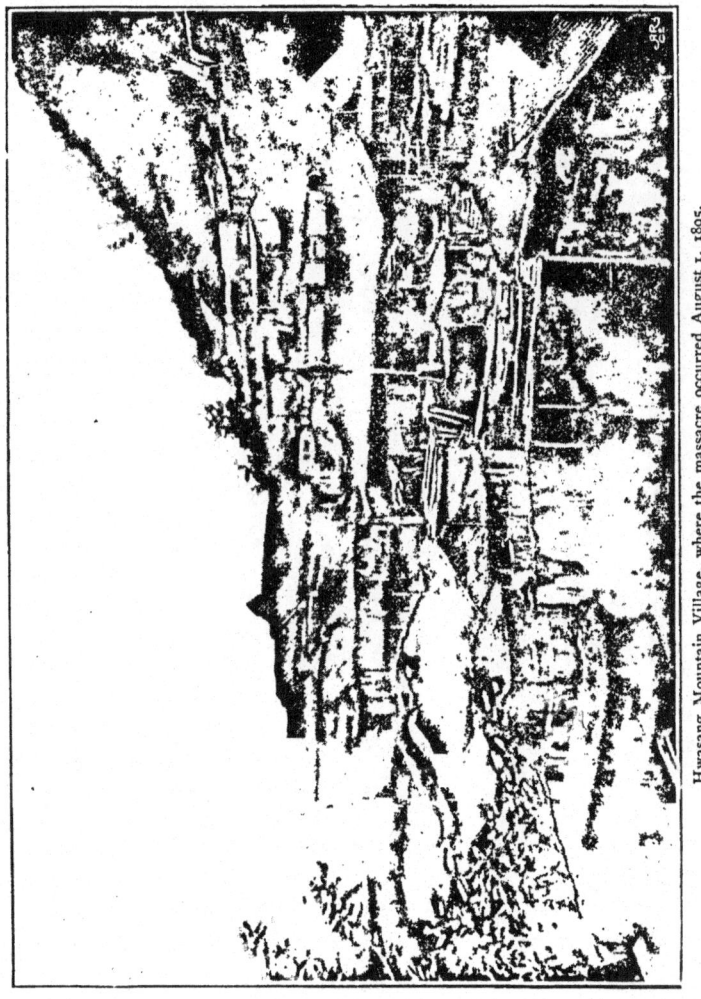

Hwasang Mountain Village, where the massacre occurred August 1, 1895.

Mr. Banister, another missionary, writes :—

" The only adult survivor of our party, Miss Codrington, there is hope of, though she has some very bad wounds.

" The blood of the martyrs has ever been the seed of the Church, and that mountain top has been consecrated by the outpoured blood of these beloved saints, that Kucheng and the whole of China may be saved. Quick and short for them was the way to glory and the eternal crown. Our hearts are torn with the agony of this bitter trial, but for them there is now the eternal joy and the eternal rest."

One of the " Sisters " writes :—

" Do pray much for China just now, and for Kucheng. It must, I fear, stop the work there for a time; but *they* loved it, and *God* loves it, and we *do* want to go back.

. . . . .

" To those of us who knew them well, their lives cannot but be an inspiration.

" On the way down a woman came to Miss Codrington and said, ' Don't think your work is over; we are all in tears for this thing that has happened.'

" Miss Codrington was taken to the Foochow Hospital to be tenderly nursed by the dear sisters who have addicted themselves to this ministry; along with the four remaining children, little Herbert having ' fallen asleep' on the journey. The baby soon followed. ' Safe in the arms of Jesus,' the sisters wrote on the little white coffin."

One of them says (what we should have known if she had not written it):—

"If love and kindness could have saved her, she would have lived."

Miss Codrington's nurse sent this beautiful message from her patient, too weak to write herself:—

"Though she received many wounds, she says she felt no pain, and she is sure the others did not; she felt only a thrill of joy to think they would all soon be in glory together."

And now my task is well-nigh over. The remaining chapters are mainly from other pens.

One word let me say to my readers. If you would follow these blessed martyrs, as they followed Christ, the steps are easy. Seek their Saviour. Admit His Holy Spirit to fill your being. Accept God's sentence of death upon all the self-life—upon what seems good, as well as upon what is manifestly bad; so that you may testify, as they did, both in life and death, "Not I, but Christ liveth in me."

CHAPTER IX

STRONG CONSOLATION

" Let them praise His Name in the dance : let them sing praises unto Him with the timbrel and harp."—Psalm cxlix. 3.

CHAPTER IX

STRONG CONSOLATION

PSALM cxlix. 3.

Lord, Thou hast loved me, and henceforth to me
  Earth's noonday is but gloom ;
My soul sails forth on the eternal sea,
  And leaves the shore of doom.

I pass within the glory even now,
  Where shapes and words are not,
For joy that passeth words, O Lord, art Thou,
  A bliss that passeth thought.

I enter there, for Thou hast borne away
  The burden of my sin ;
With conscience clear as heaven's unclouded day
  Thy courts I enter in.

Heaven now for me—for ever Christ and heaven—
  The endless NOW begun—
No *promise*—but a gift eternal *given*,
  Because the work is done.

H. SUSO.[1]

WHILE all this was happening in China, Mrs.
Stewart's mother and sisters, two of her sons,
and other relatives, were enjoying the sea breezes at
Peel, Isle of Man.

There they received the telegram that told of sudden
glory and a martyr's crown.

---

[1] In " Hymns of Tersteegen, Suso and Others."

From the very first God so comforted, by giving such vivid realization of the joy and glory of those He had taken, the survivors could not grieve.

"Thou wilt show me the path of life. In Thy presence is fulness of joy, and at Thy right hand there are pleasures for evermore," was given by God to one of them.

"Of whom the world was not worthy," was whispered by God's Spirit to the hearts of two of the company about the same time, and other messages equally beautiful but too many to enumerate here.

How blessed is it, in times like these, to have learnt to hear the Shepherd's voice !

Well might David pray, " Be not silent to me, lest if Thou be silent to me I become like those that go down to the pit."

And He has many ways in which this "mother-comforting" comes. The angels, we are told, are " all ministering spirits sent forth to minister on behalf of those who shall be heirs of salvation."

Elisha *saw* the horses and chariots of fire round about him, therefore he could not fear, though a host of mortal men had encamped against him.

When John fell down to worship at the feet of the angel he refused divine honours, telling him he was his fellow-servant, and one of those that had the testimony of Jesus.

And a second time when John again tried to worship, he was told, "I am thy fellow-servant, and of thy brethren the prophets, and of them which keep the sayings of this book : worship God."

And God hath other ways—how many and how varied we know not.

He comes through angel messengers who still abide in houses of clay, and through them He sends sweet messages of love and cheer. We quote some extracts from the many loving helpful letters received.

" Mr. Williams was with us yesterday (son of the martyr John Williams). He was touched in reading the news from China. He said he was at school in England when the dreadful news came to him, and he could recall something of what his feelings were."

" How wonderful it seems, in God's providence, that they who were so trusted and so needed should be the ones to be called like this ! "

" Truly they were His chosen ones to suffer in such a way as He honours few by asking, and what glory is theirs too."

" Your hearts must be bleeding indeed, and every heart is touched and deeply affected."

" You will have the consolation that not only our dear Lord is bearing your sorrow, but that all Christian people, the wide world over, are sharing in it, and praying for you and for those others who have lost friends in this awful riot."

" Ten thousand hearts are bleeding for you and yours to-day. But I know the Saviour is pouring in His loving sympathy and tender consolation."

" My eyes seem to rest on dear Mrs. Stewart's face, so full of Heaven as we last saw it—how full of heaven will it be when we see it again ! "

"My heart has just been full of you one and all. Even for myself it has been a greater sorrow and loss than I can tell you; few I loved and valued and admired so well as Robert and Louisa; very few I prayed for so constantly. I had such a precious half-hour with him at our C.M.S. anniversary, April, 1893, and I do feel it an honour to have dear cousin among 'the Noble Army of Martyrs.'"

"Is not John xii. 24 very precious just now? We may watch with certainty for the much fruit."

From Switzerland:—

"We well remember Mr. Stewart's visit to Torquay in 1884, when he stayed at —— and spoke at the C.M.S. meeting. What specially impressed us about him at that meeting was the utter absence of self. He never even alluded to the danger and persecutions through which they had passed, and spoke at table with such genuine love and devotion to his work."

"Dear —— was so fond of your dear sister, and used to speak of her unworldly, saintly character.

"May we not pray and hope and believe that even these things may fall out rather unto the furtherance of the Gospel, for which they have indeed laid down their lives?"

"The blood of the martyrs may be the seed of a glorious harvest, to rejoice their hearts and yours in the day of His appearing."

"Your precious ones are crowned with 'the ruby crown'; the noble army of martyrs praise Thee."

"Think of them there."

" For them sudden glory and a martyr's crown and great eternal reward."

" They can say with a smile ' Fear not them which kill the body, and after that have no more that they can do.' . . . The Lord knows whom He can trust with the heaviest trials. He knows whose faith will stand it, and He puts a high honour upon you in sending you this."

" I loved dear Mr. and Mrs. Stewart very much, and looked forward to meeting them below, but now it must be above. Have they not been faithful unto death, and theirs is the crown of life ? "

" They must have been preaching the Gospel in power so to have roused the devil."

" They will have their reward in the glory which shall be revealed in them, and in seeing China really opened to the Gospel."

" What a difference it makes to one's life to be connected with those who have been sent the martyr's crown—the highest of the heavenly awards! "

" It takes us right back to the days of the early persecutions, and forward into the glory-land at a stroke! "

" How they must rejoice! and now also, as ministering angels, must they not be engaged in comforting us with the comfort wherewith they themselves are comforted of God ? "

" I am *certain* God and China will have great victory out of this tremendous sorrow."

" One cannot realize that those saintly Stewarts are

no longer in the fight, but in the very presence of our Lord. Their very name is a blessing . . ."

"Now they have leisure to talk together of all that has happened on the way."

"Perfect divine love must have its own perfect reasons for not interfering and preventing. . . . Let our tears be praises, and let our sighs and moans turn into triumphant songs of victory before the Lamb of God, who was slain and was *the* self-sacrifice, and who by this has overcome. . . . Let us comfort one another with the thought 'The Lord is at hand.' Let us be patient. Stablish our hearts, for the coming of the Lord draweth near."

"It was *not* what it seems to us! There *was* a presence with them so bright, so encircling that they were shielded from so much *we* see ; and, or ever they were aware, the glory burst upon them."

"He redeemeth their soul from deceit and violence, and precious shall their blood be in His sight."

"Surely a blessing must follow, and the name of Jesus will be glorified. They are among the great 'cloud of witnesses.'"

From Bedford, where they lived for a short time :—

"Dear Mr. and Mrs. Stewart ! we truly loved them, as did every one who knew them. We all feel their martyrdom as a real personal sorrow. To know them was to love them. They were indeed saints on earth, ready ever to do and suffer God's will. The last conversation I think I ever had with your dear sister here in this drawing-room was on the subject of God's will.

I was so struck with the bright way she spoke! I
wish I could remember what she said, but she spoke of
loving it.

" She said, If we continually brought ourselves to
say to Him, ' I love Thy will, O Lord,' we would come
really to love it. Now they have been counted worthy
to suffer for the Saviour's sake.

" I so *often* think of her words; and we may be sure
that He was with them in their short passage from
this world."

" Miss W. wrote (from China) that my niece (Miss
Codrington) said she felt no pain from her dreadful
wounds that awful day. . . . It comforts us in
thinking of the others."

" It is very touching to hear of the four who lived
together, locking their bedroom door and praying
together, led by Hessie Newcombe, just before the men
entered their room."

From Canada :—

" Mr. and Mrs. Stewart were ideal missionaries, so
very lovely in their lives and characters, so wholly
given up to the Holy Spirit's guiding, and so used of
God. The very brightness of their faces brought
glory to God. And though their great love for each
other was so apparent, and their love for their children
and for all of you so intense, the first thought was
always the Master's will and the Master's work. The
good they did out here will never be known in this
life. Surely the Lord has some very good thing in
store for them, when He called them so quickly above,

and gave to them the honour of following so closely in His footsteps."

From Japan :—

" The news of the awful events of last week will have reached you before they reached us, and all the world over Christian people will be holding the bereaved ones in prayerful sympathy before God."

" When I told my teacher the cause of my sorrow, he immediately said, ' Let us pray '; and when a few nights after I was talking to one of our catechists and his wife about the dear children, he also said, ' Let us pray for them.' Surely this seed will bring forth a hundredfold."

. " God has chosen thy children for the rare distinction of martyrdom, for the crown that but few of our generation shall ever wear."

A prelate of the Church of Ireland writes :—

" I was preaching in a country church yesterday on John xiv. 15, and at the close I alluded to Mark xvi. 15 as an instance of a commandment, and to the death of Mr. and Mrs. Stewart. If Mrs. Smyly had seen the tears of the rough farmers present, she would have felt at all events that there is deep sympathy, and I trust there is also much prayer."

Another writes :—

" Oh ! God is getting great glory out of all this, and we do praise Him. May we be taught just now to pray for you all, and for those ' afar off ' in the widest sense of that expression."

" A friend had this text given for us the night before

he heard the news—' Why seek ye the living among the dead ? ' "

" It almost seems an intrusion to write just now, and yet I must, just to tell you how our prayers are with you. . . . God knew when His servants had finished His work ; and if He took them home by a shorter way than they expected, the rest and joy of home will more than make up for the roughness of the way.

" May I tell you a little scrap from Mr. Stewart's address at our C.M.S. meeting in 1891 ? He was speaking of suffering for Christ's sake, and telling of the persecution of two native converts. ' Remember,' he said, ' we must be ready to die. . . . Think of Jesus. Keep your eye on Him. How He suffered on the Cross for us. Though no human hand may be there to close your eyes, there will be One there *always* " all the days." " Unto me, who am less than the least of all saints, is this grace given, that I should preach among the Gentiles the unsearchable riches of Christ." '

" ' If those words are yours, your end is to be envied.' "

" We have prayed much for you all, and feel quite sure that in the midst of it all you are praising God.

" He never makes a mistake."

" Truly it is when we are passing through the waters that we really understand the Presence and the wondrous upholding."

" ' Except a corn of wheat fall into the ground and

die. . . . If it die, it bringeth forth much fruit,'
which is even already showing in the quickened
interest in Missions everywhere showing itself through
their suffering."

"God will lift you up far, very far above earth and
all earthly things to where Christ crowns His peculiarly honoured servants and handmaids. May such
an excess of faith be yours as shall enable you to see
your beloved one clearly in her new martyr joy and
glory."

Mrs. E. C. Millard tells of a letter from Australia:
that many friends there said they had seen in Mr.
Stewart's *life* the reality of what they had heard about
in meetings and services held the year before by Rev.
George Grubb and his Mission party.

From India:—

"Who ever heard her plead for China that was not
touched by her spirit and enthusiasm? That, whether
by life or death, to witness for Christ amongst the
heathen was the highest privilege in the world? And
now the joy of the Lord is theirs for evermore."

From Ceylon:—

"I shrank from putting first my first thought, which
was of the heartiest congratulations that the precious
Saviour should so honour you and yours as to enable
them to fill up the measure of ' the sufferings of Christ
for His body's sake '—the poor Chinese who shall
believe on Him through their life's testimony! He
must love those poor cruel people very much when He
allows such a precious sacrifice ' to be offered on the

service of their faith.' I keep thinking God so loved the people of Kucheng that He gave His own loved ones to prove by their lives the sincerity of their faith. Since the first telegram, which I hardly believed, I have been praying, ' Father, forgive them,' for the poor Chinese ' know not what they do.' "

From Australia :—

" We are deeply interested in the work, as Mrs. Saunders' daughters were from Kew. At first it seemed hard to think of so many useful lives sacrificed, but already it seems as if the fruit is appearing. God's ways are not our ways, but they are best, for He knows all things. There are a great many Chinese in Melbourne, and those who attend classes and meetings are in a very softened state and much impressed by this sad news. Christians are busy working among them, and the Chinese profess to be very much ashamed of their countrymen.

" A lady who went to see Mrs. Saunders found her seated between two Chinese ladies, and she was comforting them, so great was their grief. Some of the Chinese students attending a class held in connection with Kew Church, sent a message that they were too ashamed and distressed to come, but Mrs. Saunders sent back a message begging them to come as usual, as her daughters loved their people, and had given their lives for them.

" I believe what has happened will spread worldwide, and cause a great revival. We attended the memorial service held at St. Hilary's, to which the

Misses Saunders belonged. It was a very solemn time, but it was a time too of rejoicing. The service was a very impressive one, but full of deep calm joy.

" ' Faithful unto death,' was written in white flowers and palms. Great beautiful ones waved gently in the light breeze coming in at the open windows, symbols of victory and triumph.

" ' Faithful unto death,' in white flowers and palms in Australia.

" ' Faithful unto death,' on ' Lena's ' coffin in China. Yes, and the Lord has fulfilled His promise. ' I will give thee the crown of life.'

" ' Through faith they obtained promises . . they, out of weakness, were made strong, waxed valiant in fight, turned to flight the armies of the aliens.'

" To the eye of faith, this was no mere attack of Chinese people upon English missionaries.

" But the great war that is being waged all over this earth is in reality in the spiritual kingdom. The victories are spiritual, the enemies—' hosts of wicked spirits ' (Eph. 6), sometimes *in* human beings.

" The members of this fanatical sect have taken ascetic vows of abstinence from liquors, opium, tobacco, and flesh meat ; hence they are sometimes called ' Vegetarians.'

" They have vowed to stamp out the name and religion of Jesus from China, and to exterminate those who worship Him. On their banner they wrote, ' The Dragon will conquer the foreigners' God.'

" In this holy war these pioneer missionaries fell, and yet they conquered.

"God's greatest victories look to the natural eye like defeat.

" When our Saviour Jesus Christ was left, deserted by His disciples, seemingly forsaken by God; when He cried that bitter cry, ' Why hast *Thou* forsaken me?' and at last poured out His soul unto death, did it not seem to common sense as if He had been defeated, as if the devil had gained the day?

" But our defeats are God's victories. And as the Cross of Jesus will ever stand, the centre of all time, the example of pure, unselfish love, so is it the greatest example of God's triumph, in and through weakness.

" The One who knew no sin, was made sin for us that we might be made the righteousness of God in Him.

" We know God has gained a great victory in China, that from these precious lives laid down will spring up an innumerable company in China, who, together with these blessed martyrs, will praise the Lamb. Can we not say, with John, ' And I beheld, and I heard the voice of many angels round about the throne and the living creatures and the elders:

" ' And the number of them was ten thousand times ten thousand, and thousands of thousands:

" ' Saying with a loud voice, Worthy is the Lamb that was slain to receive power, and riches, and wisdom, and strength, and honour, and glory, and blessing.

" ' And every creature which is in heaven, and on the earth, and under the earth, and such as are in the sea, and all that are in them, heard I saying, Blessing and honour and glory and power be unto Him that sitteth upon the Throne, and unto the Lamb for ever and ever.

·" ' And the four living creatures said, Amen. And the four and twenty elders fell down and worshipped Him that liveth for ever and ever.' "

CHAPTER X

"CALLED, AND CHOSEN, AND FAITHFUL

Rev. xvii. 14.

CHAPTER X

THE GOLDEN CITY

REV. xxi. 11.

I have seen this golden city
    Shining as the noonday clear,
Seen the glory that surrounds it
    As of sunset drawing near,
And my soul hath caught an echo
    Of the music that resounds
Through all its woods and meadows :—
    " In this city Love abounds,
          Love abounds."

There is no night in this city,
    Here the Sun goes down no more,
For the Lord Himself unveileth
    His own Light from shore to shore ;
Where the stillness is so perfect
    In its harmony of sounds
That the soul hears but one utterance—
    " In this city Love abounds,
          Love abounds."

Christ alone is King of glory,
    He—The Lamb who once was slain !
And this wondrous living city
    Is the outcome of His pain :
'Tis His own all-glorious body,
    Hence we hear the joyful sounds

That for ever echo through it :—
" In this city Love abounds,
Love abounds."

THE STORY OF LENA THE IRISH NURSE.

L ENA was *called* by God when quite a child in one
of the Dublin Mission Homes. She heard the
call and recognised the Voice.

She was *chosen* of Him that she should be holy and
without blemish, and to her also was this grace given
that she should preach by word and life among the
heathen the unsearchable riches of Christ.

She was *faithful* even unto death. She lost her life
in seeking to save another.

When Lena was eleven years old, she knew very
distinctly that Christ had taken possession of her as
His temple, to fill with grace and glory, and thence to
bless others.

She was a bright, clever girl, and her friends
thought she would make a good teacher in one of the
Mission schools. But Lena herself had other views
in her little mind.

In the world outside the Elliott Home changes
had been taking place. Miss Louisa Smyly, a great
favourite among the Mission school children, had been
married, and had become Mrs. Robert Stewart. She
had gone out to China with her husband, followed to
her far foreign home by the love and interest of many
to whom she had been helpful in Dublin. But in one
little Elliott Home girl's heart there was a special
link of sympathy,—a God-given link.

The wise little maiden felt that if she could help forward God's work by helping Mrs. Stewart and setting *her* free to teach the Chinese women, her great wish would be fulfilled.

Some years passed by, and Mr. and Mrs. Stewart returned from China with a family of little children. In the summer holidays they went to Wales to be near the sea. Mrs. Stewart wanted a girl to help her in the care of her children. And though Lena's desires were locked up in her own little heart, the matron of the Home had *her* ideas on the same subject, feeling that her capable trustworthy pupil might be a real help to Mrs. Stewart, and she gladly recommended her for the vacant place. And Lena found herself promoted, for the time at least, to the work she had so desired.

She proved herself so faithful and useful during the temporary engagement, that the next proposal was, to her unbounded delight, that she should be permanently installed as nurse and go back to China with the family on their return. I need hardly say the offer was accepted, even with tears of joy. And from that time (with one interval of a year, when she went to stay with her mother, who had emigrated to America) the little voices that called on "Ena" for help and counsel in their daily joys and sorrows and occupations filled her life with happy, useful work.

Not without its trials ; such as the long hours when Mrs. Stewart was out among her Chinese women, and the bright young Irish girl—she was only seventeen when she went out—was left alone with her little charges, no other English-speaking person within reach. It was well that her life-path had not been lightly chosen ; and better still, that she had learned to know Him who says, " I will never leave thee."

When Mr. and Mrs. Stewart had to come home in 1888, as already stated, to recruit his health, Lena, of course, came with them. She proved to be a great comfort, not only through her watchful care of the children, but by her ready thoughtfulness and Christian sympathy.

The love she bore to Mr. and Mrs. Stewart was God's own love shed abroad in her heart by the Holy Ghost. This was proved by her unselfishness. Merely human love is an outcome of the self-life, and is never quite free from selfishness. God's love alone is like the sunshine—all give and no take.

We all counted Lena as a friend, no longer a servant merely (hallowed as that name and position is through our Saviour's life of humble service), but also a sister beloved in the Lord.

During the short happy time that they called Bedford home, I used to see Lena occasionally, and not the least important part of a few days' visit to my sister was the little time with Lena in the nursery.

One day baby *would not* sleep. And Lena had something on her heart to say, but even the hearts of babies are in the Lord's hand, and He turns them whithersoever He will. Baby slept, and Lena could tell her request for prayer. It was for blessing deep and lasting on the Y.W.C.A. in Bedford, and for special meetings about to be held.

Lena was a Y.W.C.A. member, and deeply interested in the Association.

Mrs. Stewart was made President of the Bedford Association while she was resident in that town. Lena and her mistress were always one in spirit, and they both loved the Y.W.C.A.; and I am sure they both prayed God to bless it as long as they lived.

To this union of spirit between mother and nurse we attribute much of the blessing which, through God's mercy, has been given to the children.

In all the little difficulties which always arise with a family of seven or eight children the one resource with Mrs. Stewart and Lena was prayer.

They clung to that promise, " If two of you shall agree as touching anything that they shall ask, *it shall be done.*" And the promise, or rather the Promiser, it is needless to say, never failed them.

Lena never forsook her old love for the new. China, the land of her adoption, was the new love, Ireland and her people, and specially " The Elliott Home," her own home, was the old. Every year the savings from her wages were sent to its funds. Earnestly and fervently she prayed for the children, and heartily did she thank God for the Dublin Mission Homes and Schools.

The arrangement made when Mr. and Mrs. Stewart were returning to China, in 1893, showed how highly they valued Lena's capability and trustworthiness. It was, of course, impossible to take little children on a missionary tour in Canada, so they were left to make the long journey to Foochow, in their faithful nurse's care.

How vividly we remember the start that October evening, the little travellers well wrapped up for their night journey, dear little four-year-old Herbert clinging to a stuffed calico "pussy"; and Lena moving about among them, so quiet and self-possessed, seeming to know everything, and to remember everything that was necessary.

The journey was safely accomplished, and we heard with joy of the happy meeting in China.

Since then Lena's letters have been interesting, full of nursery news, well written and well expressed.

In spare evenings Mrs. Stewart taught Lena Chinese, so that when she went out with the children she could give a simple message to the Chinese women who came in her way.

She soon learned to say, " Jesus loves you, and died to save you."

One of Lena's last letters, written in May, 1895, tells about the flight from Kucheng at the first alarm of the Vegetarians; how she packed blankets and clothes in baskets for Mrs. Stewart and the children.

She gives beautiful glimpses of the confidence and oneness of spirit between the workers whom God had joined in such close union in His work, and whom He was so soon going to gather up together into the unseen glory.

Then the letter goes back to nursery details, very touching to read now; how baby caught cold on the journey, and how her teeth were troubling her; but finally the careful nurse says, "She is quite bright again," and goes on to tell of more little plays and sayings.

Sweet, happy home-life, not ended, only carried within the veil by that wild outbreak of fanatical fury. We know how the faithful nurse went home by that rough path with two of her nurslings.

We do not want to dwell in thought on the rough path—the earthly side. It seemed as if God drew our hearts up, and taught us to say, "Lord, they are with Thee"; the little ones "quite bright again." Ah! how bright in the sunshine of Thy presence, all that band rejoicing now in the presence of the King.

> " Safe gathered home around Thy blessed feet,
>   Come home by different roads from near and far ;
>   Whether by whirlwind or by flaming car,
>   From pangs or sleep, safe folded round Thy seat."

And so we close this sketch of what God was pleased to do in living temples, where He had come to dwell. "For God hath said, I will dwell in them and walk in them."

No less in the faithful young nurse (missionary and martyr) than in the devoted mother, Louisa Stewart, —mother, not only of her own children, but of many in China and elsewhere, who loved to call her Mission

R

Mother, and Robert Stewart, father, Mission Father, beloved brother, patient humble worker, happy, blessed martyr.

Their lives still speak to us, and this is what they say:

"Wherefore come out from among them, and be ye separate, saith the Lord, and touch not the unclean thing; and I will receive you.

"And will be a Father unto you; and ye shall be my sons and daughters, saith the Lord Almighty."

Butler & Tanner, The Selwood Printing Works, Frome, and London.

CPSIA information can be obtained
at www.ICGtesting.com
Printed in the USA
BVOW03*1256061017
496953BV00008B/374/P